Adventure Guide to
Mount Rainier

A FALCON GUIDE ®

Adventure Guide to
Mount Rainier

Hiking, climbing and skiing in Mount Rainier National Park

A CHOCKSTONE PRESS BOOK

FALCON®

HELENA, MONTANA

Jeff Smoot

ADVENTURE GUIDE TO MOUNT RAINIER

FRONT COVER: Mount Rainier by Alan Kearney.
BACK COVER: top photo by Alan Kearney; bottom photo by Rob Lovitt.

ISBN 1-56044761-3

PUBLISHED AND DISTRIBUTED BY:
Falcon® Publishing, Inc.
P.O. Box 1718
Helena, Montana 59624

Preface

There are already many guidebooks to Mount Rainier and the National Park bearing its name. These guides discuss roads, trails, viewpoints, visitor services, geology, glaciers, wildflowers, wildlife, forests communities and park history, to name only a few of many subjects. Other guides include Mount Rainier only as part of a larger subject, whether climbing, hiking or skiing. Ruth Kirk's guide, Exploring Mount Rainier, originally published in 1977, has disappeared from bookstores and is out of print. It offered an introduction to Mount Rainier for the tourist and casual adventurer, encouraging visitors to get out of their cars and hike to waterfalls, meadows and scenic vistas. But, even so, it was intended more for tourist hikers, and offered little or nothing for alpine scramblers, climbers or skiers.

This guide goes a step beyond Exploring Mount Rainier, providing useful information for almost any Mount Rainier National Park adventure. This is a "user's guide" to the mountain, not a looker's guide. Climbing, hiking, scrambling, skiing and snowshoeing, among other activities, all under one cover. It is hoped this guide will be a useful source of information for any Mount Rainier excursion, from a two-week hike on the Wonderland Trail to a weekend summit climb, to an afternoon hike, and everything in between. The guide won't tell you everything; its purpose is to show you how to get there so you can see it all for yourself. It is merely a starting point for your explorations of Mount Rainier National Park.

Obviously, even so ambitious a project will not be entirely comprehensive. There remain many trailless areas of the park best left for private exploration. Some magnificent and memorable hikes, as well as off-trail, climbing and ski routes are described in a mere sentence, some not at all. Many were omitted due to environmental concerns, others because of lack of space. However, just because a trail or peak isn't listed in this book doesn't mean it's unworthy of your attention. If this guide described every square mile of the park, it would be much too voluminous, and would surely eliminate any sense of adventure for those who seek it here.

During the course of writing this guide, I became aware of the need for conservancy by wilderness visitors. Most visitors are not aware that 97% of the park is designated wilderness, and as such requires special care. Most wilderness users – hikers, climbers, skiers and scramblers – take care to minimize their impact. However, with the thousands who come to Mount Rainier's wilderness areas each year, and the resultant overuse and abuse of some of the park's best subalpine meadows and alpine environments, there is much room for improvement. The Park Service estimates that 200,000 day hikers, 12,000 backpackers and 7,000 climbers visit Mount Rainier's wilderness each year, a number that is growing. I cannot deny that guidebooks, such as this one, are partly responsible for the crush of visitors to our wilderness areas. But there are already

Table of Contents

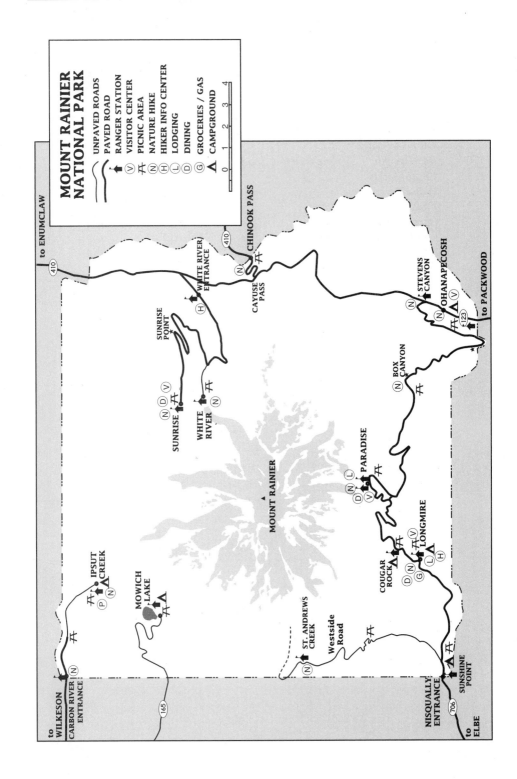

Introduction

Webster's Ninth New Collegiate Dictionary defines "adventure" as "to expose to danger or loss . . . to venture . . . to proceed despite risk." The word "adventure" has various synonyms, including daring, daredevil, rash, reckless, foolhardy, etc. This guide, then, is by definition a guide to daring, reckless or foolhardy acts that will expose you to danger and risk. However, this guide is written with another meaning of the word adventure also in mind: "an exciting or remarkable experience." The exposure to risks and dangers is partly what makes adventures exciting and remarkable, and thus so appealing to the adventuresome. If we don't know the outcome in advance, we are much more greatly rewarded by the experience.

To maintain your sense of adventure in exploring Mount Rainier National Park, routes included in this guide will be described and illustrated in a manner that will lead you to your objectives without giving away every detail. Some routes have detailed drawings and photographs; some are left vague by necessity, if only to force you to figure things out for yourself and, thus, have an adventure instead of a commonplace experience. If this guide told you every move to make and every step to take, or otherwise guaranteed your success and enjoyment, you surely would miss out. Real adventure begins where the trail ends, well beyond this guide's descriptions and illustrations, when you search for what lies above and beyond.

Using This Guide

This guide does not presume to know every feature of every peak, valley, glacier, stream, trail or road in Mount Rainier National Park. Mountain environments change from day to day, week to week, season to season, year to year. Minor rockfalls, ice avalanches, floods – even weather and seasonal changes – will continually alter the nature and course of mountain routes. Trails erode, streams and rivers flood, bridges are washed out, trees fall, crevasses open and close, seracs tumble, ice cliffs avalanche, glaciers recede and advance, and, perhaps someday, Mount Rainier will again erupt. Because mountain features can change, hiking trails and cross-country and climbing routes will vary accordingly. A feature identified in a route description herein may have changed or disappeared between the time of this writing and the time you are looking for it. Changes can and do occur overnight. Be prepared!

Each section of the guide contains maps showing roads, trails and other routes and points of interest. You should not rely on these maps except to the extent that they will help guide you to your chosen destination from the lowlands. Although these maps may suffice for competent persons during good weather, they are not exact, and cannot substitute for topographic maps, skilled compass use, and routefinding ability learned through experience. U.S. Geological Survey 7½-minute series maps used to develop this book

Throughout the book, these symbols are used to designated different types of trails on maps:

- ⑫ Hiking Trails
- ⑫ Off-trail Routes
- ⑫ Winter Routes

include Golden Lakes, Mount Wow, Mowich Lake, Mount Rainier West, Mount Rainier East, Sunrise, White River Park and Chinook Pass; these would be useful to the adventurer who needs more detail on any route.

Photographs with overlays are used to show features and climbing routes on Mount Rainier. Like maps, photographs should not be relied upon completely, although they may give you a helpful perspective of Mount Rainier and its features. Use your best judgment on each route regardless of the written descriptions, illustrations and photographic overlays contained in this guide.

Routes in this guide are, in most cases, described beginning from the Nisqually Entrance and proceeding counterclockwise around Mount Rainier. Easier and more-popular routes will receive a more thorough discussion mostly because parties taking these routes are usually less experienced and may need more detail. Technical and infrequently traveled routes will be discussed in sufficient detail to allow you to approach and locate the routes. Basically, this guide will show you what's there and approximately where to go; from there it's up to you.

With the exception of maintained trails, the routes listed in this guide are approximate only, and are based upon historical and popular usage. Numerous variations to these routes have been and will be done, whether for the sake of something different or to avoid occasional hazards or obstacles, and all of these variations cannot possibly be known, let alone listed here. For most of the routes in this guide, there is no "correct" or absolute route. There are no dotted lines to follow on the mountains (thank goodness); you'll have to pick the best and safest route by yourself.

All route descriptions and directions assume you are facing Mount Rainier and/or your direction of travel, unless otherwise stated. All distances, including road and trail mileages, are approximate.

Alpine Zone camp and bivouac sites mentioned in the text and shown on maps and photographs are suggested or previously used sites only, and are not guaranteed to be safe or even comfortable. Officially designated trailside camps are presumed to be at least moderately safe and comfortable, and most are near a year-round water source.

A large part of the Mount Rainier experience, as with any wilderness travel, is discovery and exploration. In that spirit, this guide won't give away all of the surprises. This is not a fully-illustrated instruction book for preassembled adventures; rather, it is a starting point for those who wish to discover and explore Mount Rainier National Park. Those who wish to be guided every step of the way may consult other guides listed in the bibliography for further details. Hopefully, however, users of this guide will learn how to get where they are going, but won't miss out on the best part of the outdoor experience – the adventure – in the process.

Mountain Hazards

Mountaineering and wilderness travel have numerous objective dangers, and routes described in this guide are no exceptions. Hikers and climbers venturing into the backcountry – and especially the trailless areas of Mount Rainier National Park – subject themselves to numerous hazards. Despite all of the obvious potential dangers, thousands of backcountry trips are made each year without incident or injury. However, we shouldn't be too smug about this, especially on Mount Rainier. There are no guarantees of safety in the backcountry, so proceed with caution, and at your own risk.

This guide will make an effort to point out obvious objective hazards. Warnings in this guide are intended to let users know of dangers that frequently are encountered on given routes. Hiking on trails is the safest mode of backcountry travel, where usually only weather and your own or others' actions are reasons for concern. When venturing off the trail, you subject yourself to greater risks, including but not limited to avalanches, rockfall, icefall, windfall, landslides, lightning strikes, floods, jökulhlaups, slips and falls, crevasses, frostbite and effects of weather and volcanic eruption, along with the ordinary hazards of being human. Unfortunately, no one can predict most of these occurrences, as even the weatherman cannot always predict the coming of a major storm. You should be wary of these dangers at all times, and avoid them whenever possible. Indeed, climbers often are the cause their own and others' accidents. To follow certain routes, however, one must be willing to face certain risks. Once again, this guidebook is no substitute for good judgment or experience. It will try to warn you away from obvious and foreseeable hazards, but there are always potential hazards lurking out there that nobody knows about until it is too late.

Wear a Helmet!

Climbers and scramblers attempting any route that passes over, beneath, near or through volcanic rock gullies and cliffs, or anywhere else stonefall or icefall might occur, are advised to wear helmets. The rock in Mount Rainier National Park mostly is very poor, and disintegrates with little provocation. Rocks, icicles and ice chunks regularly pelt climbers on Mount Rainier without warning. Granted, a helmet won't protect you from 2.6 million cubic yards of avalanching volcanic debris, but it might save your life if you get hit in the head by a more typical fist-sized stone or icicle. Helmets are recommended on all climbs and scrambles, but mostly on those with potential for rock or ice fall.

You should check weather and avalanche conditions before each trip. Make sure you and your entire party have adequate experience for and knowledge of your chosen routes, both for ascent and descent. If conditions become dangerous, for any reason, or you realize your chosen route is beyond your ability, don't be afraid to turn back – it is wiser than to continue in such instances.

As illustrated in this picture, helmets help keep skulls intact. (Photo: Howard Weaver)

Jökulhlaups and Debris Flows

Jökulhlaups (the Icelandic name for glacial outburst floods) and debris flows are a very real danger to those who find themselves in the wrong creek or river channel at the wrong time. Most jökulhlaups on Mount Rainier are thought to begin when heavy rainfall or snow melt water trapped within a glacier is released suddenly and rushes down a stream channel, wiping out everything within its narrow path and carrying debris, including tree limbs and boulders, along for the ride. Debris flows often are caused by heavy precipitation runoff in unstable drainage channels. Research indicates that debris flows are more common than jökulhlaups on Mount Rainier, although both may do similar damage. Look at the Tahoma and Kautz Creek drainage channels, and at the remains of the old Nisqually River bridge (just upriver from the present bridge) for evidence of the destructive power of outburst floods and debris flows. If you are in or near a creek or river drainage fed by Mount Rainier's glaciers, and hear a sudden rumbling noise coming from upstream, get to high ground fast! You can't outrun a jökulhlaup or debris flow. Don't camp near any glacier-fed streams or rivers, except at designated and approved campsites, which presumably are safe from such dangers.

A lowland forest stream along the Wonderland Trail. (Photo: Rob Lovitt)

Mountain Weather

Weather is not always poor in the Pacific Northwest, even if it seems that way. Seattle, considered "rainy" by most standards, is said to have a lower average annual rainfall than New York City. However, the Pacific Northwest's reputation for precipitation is not entirely unfounded. Washington's Olympic Peninsula has one of the highest measured annual rainfall totals in the nation. The slopes of Mount Rainier have seen world-record snowfalls, and are host to a rare, inland temperate rainforest. When it rains in the Northwest, it usually is a steady drizzle lasting several days, hence our reputation for rain.

In a nutshell, this is how Cascade mountain weather works: Warm, moist air blows in off the Pacific Ocean, squeezing moisture-laden clouds against the mountains. These clouds, like large sponges, dump excessive rain on the western slopes of the mountains and, relieved of their burden, they rise over the mountains, dissipating as they drift eastward. This warm, moist marine air condenses and freezes very rapidly when it hits a glaciated volcano, which accounts for high winds and the tremendous snowfalls each year at Mount Rainier. Because the clouds lose most of their moisture on the west side of the mountains, including Mount Rainier, the eastern slopes of the Cascade Range often lie in a protected "rainshadow." This may a bit simplistic, but it is accurate enough.

Of all considerations of mountain travel in Mount Rainier National Park, weather should be among the foremost to backcountry travelers. Many a day has began calm and clear only to end in a monsoon-like storm. Effects of weather lead to more deaths (most oftenfrom hypothermia) than climbing accidents. It has been said that Mount Rainier creates its own weather. In some respects, this is true. Weather on Mount Rainier can be remarkably different than lowland weather. This icy mountain rises into the upper atmosphere, showing the effects of incoming weather patterns more dramatically than at lower elevations. Thus, though it may be warm and calm in Seattle, Mount Rainier may have very high winds and freezing temperatures. Drizzly days at Tacoma may see several feet of snow deposited on Mount Rainier. Often, low clouds may settle over the Puget Sound region, obscuring Mount Rainier from below, while the high meadows and glaciers bask in sunlight. Chinook storms often bring winds in excess of 100 mph and despoit several feet of snow in a very short time. Mount Rainier experiences severe storms each year, and these storms cannot always be predicted, often coming without any warning, sometimes with fatal consequences. Prepare yourself for the worst, including wind, rain and snow, no matter what the weatherman says.

Lenticular cloud caps, the unmistakeable curved or lense-shaped clouds often seen hovering (like "a galactic stack of pancakes," according to one observer) over Mount Rainier, frequently form on or near the summit, sometimes obscuring the mountain's upper slopes. These clouds are formed when the expansive warm marine jet stream impacts the dense cold mountain air. These clouds usually are accompanied by very high winds and much moisture, and their formation is best interpreted as a warning to climbers to descend immediately. Lenticular clouds sometimes disperse as quickly as they form, but more often they fully engulf the mountain in raging wind and snow, sometimes depositing

A lenticular cloud caps Mount Rainier. (Photo: U. S Geological Survey)

several feet of snow over several hours or days. When a lenticular cloud settles in on Mount Rainier, it is best to descend. Although it may be disappointing to have turned back because of a lenticular cloud that dissipates just as you reach base camp, it is better than having continued your ascent into a full-on storm that can leave you stranded near the summit in high winds and extreme cold and avalanche conditions.

Winter climbers should be prepared for the worst weather imaginable. Fierce storms, with high winds and volumes of snowfall, can rage for days on Mount Rainier, and sometimes come without much warning. Plan winter climbs as you would an ascent of Mount Everest during the monsoon season, because winter weather on Mount Rainier won't be very much different. "Winter" storms can and do occur throughout the year, even in summer months, so be prepared throughout the year.

Check the weather forecast and avalanche conditions before any backcountry trip in Mount Rainier National Park. Although the weatherman is not always right about good weather, when it comes to poor weather, you should give him the benefit of the doubt, considering your life may be in the bargain. A 24-hour information line for weather, trail and road conditions (and available park services) may provide this information. You can call (360) 569-2343, or the National Park Information Desk at (360) 569-2211. Avalanche hazard and snow information may be obtained by calling the Park Service, or these hotlines: (206) 526-6677 (Washington Cascades) or (503) 326-2400 (Mount Hood and Southern Washington Cascades). Weather and avalanche forecasts and climbing conditions can be found on the Mount Rainier National Park homepage, **www.nps.gov/mora/**.

Clothing and Equipment

Although park visitors traveling in cars rarely need to worry about what to wear, anyone visiting the backcountry areas of Mount Rainier National Park must make clothing a primary consideration. It has been suggested that the only clothing modern hikers and climbers need is Gore-tex. However, as a practical and economic matter, wool clothing works fine in the rainy Cascades, as it retains some body heat even when wet. Cotton clothing certainly is more comfortable than wool, but when wet, cotton is worthless and can be deadly. Modern synthetics (like polypropylene) are said to have the same heat-retaining quality of wool with the comfort of cotton, making them a popular substitute for the heavy, scratchy wool garments most of us remember, provided raintight outer garments are worn in poor weather.

Rain- and wind-proof outer garments are a must for any mountain travel. Gore-tex and other "waterproof" fabrics are excellent at repelling water and wind, but are very expensive. A plastic poncho or less-expensive all-weather parka may suffice for those who can't afford the high-tech clothing. For climbers, a warm, insulated parka is recommended, since it usually is very cold at 3 a.m., when most parties are on the glaciers. Hikers and other visitors should wear several light layers of clothing, which may be shed or donned as the temperature rises or falls. Lug-soled, water-tight boots also are recommended for all backcountry travelers, although modern lightweight boots are becoming more popular. Advanced climbers often wear different boots for different routes, with lightweight plastic boots popular for mixed and sustained technical climbing. For most others, a lightweight multi-purpose boot will do. Make sure your boots are watertight, unless you enjoy wet, shrivelled or frozen feet.

Mittens or gloves and a warm hat are important accessories for all backcountry travel. Always bring sunglasses to keep out harmful light rays during any snow or high-elevation travel. Gaiters are recommended for any snow travel. Sunscreen often is overlooked but is as

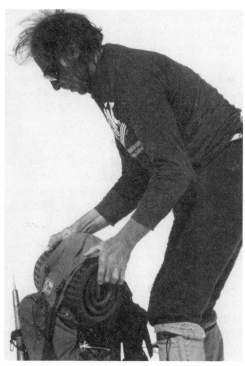

Ice axes, crampons and other gear may be essential for an excursion onto Rainier. (Photo: Mark Dale)

important for your skin as sunglasses are for your eyes, particularly for extended snow and high-elevation travel.

Winter climbers will need expedition-quality clothing, including winter parkas, overboots and mitts. Clothing for a winter ascent of Mount Rainier should be what you would wear on an ascent of Mount Everest, because conditions may be about the same. Frostbite is a real possibility for any winter or high-altitude travel, so do all you can to keep your extremities warm and dry.

The point of bringing proper clothing is to keep yourself warm and dry in a hostile mountain environment. While it may be possible and enjoyable to hike or climb in shorts and a t-shirt on perfect, warm, windless days, there have been many hypothermia deaths attributed to backcountry travelers wearing casual clothing. Dress properly and prepare for the worst; your well-being may depend on it.

Anyone venturing onto steep snow (including early season hikers) should carry and know how to use an ice ax. Crampons are necessary for all glacier travel and ice climbing, and may be useful for snow travel. A rope is highly recommended for all glacier travel and technical climbing, and one should be carried even on non-technical scrambling routes, for safety. For steep, exposed snow climbing, snow flukes and pickets make excellent belay anchors and even good intermediate protection points when placed properly. For technical routes requiring the use of pitons, you should bring a small but comprehensive rack, including a few pitons, some chocks or Friends, or whatever you prefer. For technical ice, bring whichever ice tools, ice screws and other gear suits you.

Climbing equipment will be suggested generally where it may be needed in the following chapters; however, gear lists will not be provided. You'll have to rely on your own experience and judgment when selecting the clothing and climbing equipment to bring with you. Most importantly, you need to know how to use the stuff before you venture onto Mount Rainier and its surrounding peaks. Any equipment's usefulness is wholly dependent upon its user's skill and knowledge.

Wilderness Safety

This guide contains many safety and common sense considerations for all wilderness travel within Mount Rainier National Park. Safety is a primary consideration for visitors venturing into Mount Rainier National Park's wilderness. Granted, any wilderness adventure is going to include exposure to risks and dangers. However, all backcountry travelers, including hikers, scramblers, wanderers, climbers, skiers and snowshoers, should read this guide thoroughly before venturing into the park's backcountry, to become aware of some of the things that might help minimize exposure to needless risk.

The safety suggestions contained in this book are only that: suggestions. Even if you follow these suggestions, your safety cannot be absolutely guaranteed. This is not an instruction book for hiking, climbing or skiing. The author and publisher cannot be responsible for the consequences of your acts while traveling to or within Mount Rainier National Park. It is assumed that those following the routes and trails listed in this guide will be experienced in wilderness travel, properly trained and equipped to safely complete their chosen route, and able to recognize and avoid the many avoidable dangers that may lurk in the backcountry.

When driving the park's roads, in addition to following common safety rules, drivers should slow down, keep their eyes on the road and their hands on the wheel. If you wish to view the scenery, pull off into a scenic turnout and then look about. Inattention behind the wheel is the leading cause of auto accidents nationwide; concentration is especially important in the park. Winter driving has its own safety considerations, which are discussed in Chapter Eight.

Keep in mind that the wilderness areas of the park are no place for the unprepared and uninitiated. Think twice before hiking too far into the backcountry, especially in poor weather. It is very easy to get lost if you can't see where you are going, or don't have a trail to follow, and if you aren't properly dressed or equipped, you are inviting trouble. Don't venture onto glaciers unless you are roped up, have an ice axe and crampons, and know how to effect a crevasse rescue. Don't try for the summit unless you have previous

Climbers ascend Tokaloo Spire. (Photo: National Park Service)

glacier climbing experience and equipment, or are in the company of a climbing guide. Don't climb rock cliffs or mountains if you don't have rock climbing experience and equipment; most of the park's rock is quite loose and is, therefore, not very good for climbing. Don't even go hiking if you aren't prepared for changes in weather or minor emergencies or injuries that may occur.

Most importantly, know your limitations. Think before you act, lest you suffer the consequences of a rash or foolish act. When in doubt, turn around and go home.

Climbing Route Classification

Some climbing and scrambling routes listed in this guide will be rated using a modified National Climbing Classification System rating scheme. Those unfamiliar with this rating system are likely unfamiliar with technical rock climbing and should not climb routes thus rated. Here is a generalized description:

- Class 1 generally is unexposed, easy scrambling or off-trail hiking, where use of hands is infrequent and there is little risk of serious injury;
- Class 2 is easy scrambling with some exposure, where you could be killed or seriously injured if you fell, but you aren't likely to fall off unless you make a serious blunder;
- Class 3 is more difficult scrambling with serious exposure, on which some climbers will want the safety of a rope, and on which an unroped fall would likely be fatal;
- Class 4 is very difficult scrambling where use of a rope is mandatory for all but the foolish and the very experienced (the leader will climb mostly unprotected, but everyone else will have the security of a top rope);
- Class 5 is technical rock climbing requiring the use of intermediate protection to shorten the length of possible (and sometimes imminent) leader falls.

Some routes may require direct aid; these will be signified by an "A" prior to a numerical designation of difficulty (e.g., A3); A1 is easy, A2 is harder, A3 harder still, A4 extreme and A5 the ultimate in aid-climbing difficulty. Fortunately, there are no routes harder than A3 listed in this guide. If you don't have prior experience with direct aid climbing, avoid it here! The same goes for glacier climbing, Class 2 and 3 scrambling, and Class 4 and 5 climbing. No climbing or scrambling route contained in this guide is appropriate for the inexperienced, unless in the company of an experienced leader or qualified guide.

The problem with this rating system, when applied to Mount Rainier in particular, is that one person's Class 3 is another person's Class 4, and one person's Class 4 is another's Class 5. Individual interpretations of ratings make any rating contained in any guide approximate at best; that is true for this guide. On volcanoes in particular, the nature of the rock and prevailing snow and ice conditions make any definitive difficulty rating suspect. These are not bolted technical rock routes, rated to absolute decimal accuracy. Ratings can change depending upon route and weather conditions. Ratings in this guide are provided only to let you know what you might encounter, and not as a guarantee of what awaits you.

The Roman numeral grading system commonly used in other climbing guides will be used here only for truly technical routes. Grades I, II and III denote technical climbs that may take a few hours to much of a day. A Grade IV climb can take all day; Grade V may require a bivouac. On any Grade III, IV and V route, be prepared for a bivouac and technical climbing; be "up" for the difficulties you will encounter. An unprepared party on a Grade V route on Mount Rainier is asking for it! The technical grades listed in this guide apply only to the technical portions of routes, and not for any part of the route that is only glacier hiking, unroped scrambling or route of descent.

In Case of Emergency

To report a backcountry or climbing accident, or any other emergency, call 911. Realistically, if you are coming out of the backcountry, try to find a park ranger who can report the accident and better assess the kind of response or evacuation required. If the situation is less critical, or you don't feel it is an emergency worthy of dialing 911, contact the nearest park ranger or call (360) 569-2211. Pay phones within the park list other numbers to call in case of emergency. Roving rangers can report emergencies via two-way radio. Many hikers and climbers carry cellular phones to report emergencies.

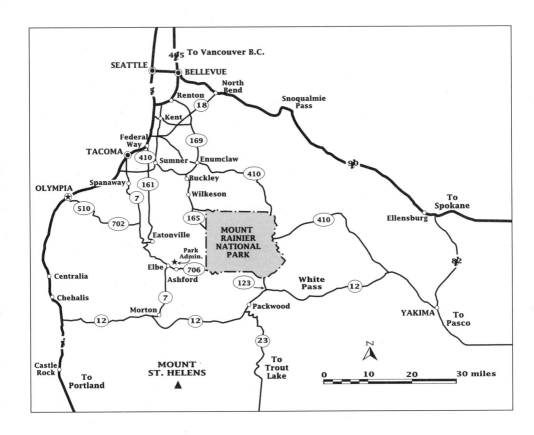

Mount Rainier National Park
and Surrounding Area

Chapter One:
The Mountain

Mount Rainier is without question the monarch of Washington's Cascade range. Certainly, the other peaks have their charms, but Rainier stands supreme in the hearts and minds of all who view it from near or afar. It is the highest volcano in the contiguous United States. The mountain was, for many years, measured at 14,410 feet of altitude, but in 1989, a satellite measurement added just over one foot to that height. Regardless, Mount Rainier is king of the Cascades. It stands out so high above surrounding peaks (about 8,000 feet higher) that it is visible from more than 100 miles away. At this height, and due to its proximity to the Pacific Ocean (only about 100 mi./175 km distant), Mount Rainier truly creates its own weather. Rising high into the thinning atmosphere, Mount Rainier stands directly in the path of prevailing moisture-laden marine winds, which results in unusual weather that seems unique to the mountain, including lenticular clouds that sometimes settle on the summit for several days while the remainder of the sky is clear. This proximity to wet marine air accounts for the high volume of snowfall on Mount Rainier. Indeed, Paradise, on the mountain's southern slope (elevation 5,400 feet), has had world-record snowfalls, and Paradise Inn often is buried in winter up to its three-story roof (early-summer guests commonly enter the Inn via a snow tunnel).

Mount Rainier's Glaciers

Mount Rainier is home to many of the largest glaciers in the contiguous United States, with 26 individual glaciers spread over 35 square miles. Six glaciers – the Emmons, Ingraham, Kautz, Nisqually, Winthrop and Tahoma – flow from the summit ice cap. There are numerous cirque-borne glaciers, including the Emmons Glacier, which has the largest surface area of any glacier in the lower 48 states, and the Carbon Glacier, whose terminus reaches the lowest elevation of any glacier in the contiguous United States. Inter glaciers – intervening glaciers formed only by snowfall accumulation – also are abundant on Mount Rainier.

Glaciers are formed when more snow accumulates during successive winters than melts away each summer. The resulting mass of snow builds up, compacts, and when it attains sufficient slope and mass, is pulled down the mountainside by gravity. Glaciers are slow movers; objects lost in crevasses sometimes are revealed at the foot of the glacier decades later. Like nature's bulldozers, glaciers tear into the soft flanks of Mount Rainier, slowly grinding it down. (Actually, it is rocks trapped by the glacier that do the scouring; the glacier simply transports the material.) The effects of glaciation are obvious: the Carbon Glacier has worn out Willis Wall; the Emmons and Winthrop Glaciers have cut the knife-edge of Steamboat Prow; the Emmons and Ingraham Glaciers have done the same to Little Tahoma Peak; rock scouring is evident at Box Canyon and other places within the park; and the Emmons and Winthrop Glaciers are undercutting

Crevasses split the ice of Winthrop Glacier. (Photo: National Park Service)

their retaining ridges, resulting in mass wasting on an enormous scale. Glaciers pick up rock debris, which speeds up the erosive process. Glaciers are transporters of tons of material, pushing, swallowing or carrying mountain debris and depositing it in terminal and lateral moraines as they crawl along.

The most important glacial features to mountain travelers are crevasses. Crevasses are simply stress fractures in the ice, and they are the most common obstacle and hazard encountered on glaciers. Although glacier ice is semi-flexible, and can bend over, around and through obstacles, it rarely does so without breaking. The more abrupt the turn or differential in glacier velocity, the more fractures will be formed. Some crevasses are formed simply from the glacier pulling down the mountainside. The curved crevasses typically seen in the middle of a glacier are formed by the differential in the rate of descent of the middle of the glacier compared to its sides. Crevasses also form where the angle of descent changes. If the angle is too severe, the glacier will likely break completely, sending huge chunks of ice avalanching down the peak and leaving "hanging" ice cliffs, such as those found atop Willis Wall on Mount Rainier. Undulations in the mountain surface will cause an overriding glacier to buckle and crack. Glaciers squeezed through narrow corridors often shatter into nearly impassable, dangerous icefalls.

Mount Rainier's glaciers keep the mountain stark white year round, adding to its impressive domination of the horizon. The icy giant hovers over Seattle and Tacoma and other Puget Sound communities, and sometimes is mistaken by newcomers as a solitary cloud on the horizon. However, Mount Rainier's mantle of ice belies its fiery origins.

The Volcano

Mount Rainier is a stratovolcano, or "composite volcano," which was built up by intermittent eruptions occuring over a long span of time. Stratovolcanos, including Rainier's closest neighbors, Mount Adams, Mount Hood and Mount St. Helens, and its many more-distant relatives along the "Pacific Rim of Fire" are built of various materials (e.g., andesite, dacite, rhyolite, ash, tuffs, basalt) piled upon each other, resulting in high, fairly uniformly-shaped masses that have been reshaped by subsequent volcanic activity and glaciation. Although not the most massive of the Cascade volcanoes, Mount Rainier is certainly the most awesome. Geologists estimate Mount Rainier is between 750,000 and one million years old.

Although Pacific Rim volcanoes do occasionally erupt explosively, most eruptions are comparatively mild, involving the expulsion of steam and ash. Needless to say, during such eruptions, it is best to stay away from the mountains. Warming and shifting of glaciers can trigger massive outburst floods (jökulhlaups) and mudslides (lahars), or break glaciers apart, and earthquakes can occur that may cause rockfall, icefall or snow avalanches. Based on data gleaned from the Mount St. Helens eruption cycle, geologists now feel confident that they can predict a major eruption, or at least give accurate warning of a potential eruption of a volcano. However, volcano eruption predictions are about as useful as weather predictions. If Mount Rainier ever starts blowing steam and ash, stay away.

Mount Rainier volcano formed atop an accumulation of several more massive, lateral andesitic flows. Many of these early, more erosion-resistant flows remain somewhat intact as Mount Rainier's intervening ridges (e.g., Rampart and Emerald Ridges). Much of the park's columnar andesite, such as that found on Emerald Ridge, Colonnade Ridge, Rampart Ridge, and at other locations, provides ample evidence of many ancient lava flows. Within the past one million years or so, Mount Rainier erupted and began building upon the base provided by earlier flows. Geologists speculate that Mount Rainier eventually rose to over 16,000 feet in elevation, but that a subsequent violent eruption, possibly similar to that of neighboring Mount St. Helens in 1980, or a caldera collapse as

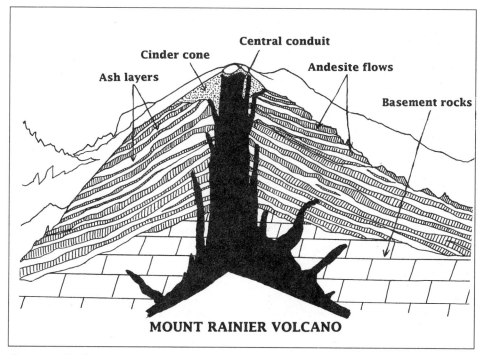

MOUNT RAINIER VOLCANO

Conceptualized cross-section of the Mount Rainier volcano.

occured on Mounts Mazama and Tehama, reduced the summit cone by over 2,500 feet, leaving a wide crater that later was filled in by other eruptions to form the present cone and smaller craters that now make up the summit area of Mount Rainier. Two of these craters are easily identified; the true summit, "Columbia Crest," is the pumice ridge dividing the two main craters.

Mount Rainier has been predominately dormant during recorded history, but it is by no means extinct. The fumaroles that warmed Stevens and Van Trump on their first ascent of the peak still spew steam from the summit-crater firn caves. Heat fluctuations within the mountain sometimes cause the melting of glacial ice and heating of mud-like volcanic rock, producing devastating mud flows. Indeed, mudflows have been singled out by geologists as the greatest volcanic threat to nearby lowland populations. The Osceola Mudflow of about 6,000 years ago buried what are present-day Enumclaw and Puyallup under a thick layer of volcanic concrete. More recently, the Nisqually, Kautz and South Tahoma Glaciers have discharged mudflows and outburst floods, and Tahoma Creek is often awash in debris flows from the Tahoma Glacier.

The threat of a volcanic eruption is ever-present, but based upon data gleaned from the eruptive cycle of Mount St. Helens in 1980, it is unlikely that a volcanic eruption will come as a complete surprise. Still, if you witness unusual steam or ash emissions from Mount Rainier, or feel earth tremors, you are well advised to find out what is going on, in case there is a real danger of an eruption or other volcanic activity.

Mount Rainier may erupt again someday, perhaps during our lifetimes. Although it is most likely that such an eruption would be nothing more than a steam outburst, it is possible that the mountain could erupt explosively. If so, its potential for devastation would be many times greater than that of Mount St. Helens during its 1980 eruption. The mudflows that choked the Toutle River after Mount St. Helens blew would be repeated, possibly down the Nisqually or White River, and into highly-populated areas bordering the mountain. For now, however, the mountain reigns with a benevolent presence, permitting us to live within its domain and approach to its very summit without fear of immediate harm.

History and Exploration

The earliest human visitors to the parklands surrounding Mount Rainier were local Indians. Indians regarded "Tahkoma" as a great spirit that spewed smoke and fire from a burning lake at its summit. Most were afraid to come near it for fear that they would be struck dead. Native inhabitants throughout the northwest had a similar respect for other Cascade volcanoes. Indian stories about the volcanoes were mostly mythical explanations of volcanic eruptions. A well-known legend is of a "tomanowas man" who, upon advice of his totem, climbed into Mount Rainier's summit crater in search of "hiaqua" (shell money), which he found there. However, having failed to make an offering to the great spirit Sahalie, he is stranded on the mountain for about 30 years, whereafter he returns to his wife and leads an honest life.

The first historic sighting of Mount Rainier was by Captain George Vancouver in 1792. He named the snowy giant after his friend, Rear Admiral Peter Rainier. That name was the subject of considerable debate later on, since Rear Admiral Rainier had fought against colonists in the American Revolution. Nearby residents, most notably those living in Tacoma, Washington, wanted the "native" name "Takhoma" replaced. One scheme would have renamed all the Cascade volcanoes for former United States Presidents; however, only Mount Adams got a presidential moniker. The main proponent of the plan, Hall J. Kelley, "ran out of ex-presidents' names and, therefore, did not depose Mount Rainier." House Concurrent Resolution No. 8, January 1917, officially laid the matter to rest, proclaiming, "'Tacoma' is not an Indian word, and never was the Indian name of Mount Rainier." In actuality, Indians had many names for Mount Rainier, including Duk-hwahk, Pus-ke-house, Ta-co-bud and Tiswauk, and apparently even the disputed Takhoma.

Ironically, the first "white men" to visit Mount Rainier were led to the mountain by local Indians, who apparently were willing to trade their fear of the mountain for a fee. Early explorers included Dr. William F. Tolmie who, in the summer of 1833, ventured into what is now the northwestern portion of the park in the company of two Indian guides. Tolmie, on a botanical journey, apparently climbed Hessong Rock (above what is now Spray Park), although Tolmie Peak, several miles distant, bears his name. In 1841, Lieutenant Charles Wilkes' survey party visited the area and calculated the height of Mount Rainier to be 12,330 feet high. One Yakima Indian guide, Saluskin (or Sluskin, but not Sluiskin, who will be mentioned later), led early explorers into the White River area in the early 1850s; this group may have made a partial ascent of the Emmons Glacier. It also is possible that Colonel Benjamin Franklin Shaw ascended Mount Rainier in August 1854. Although accounts admit Shaw and his companions, Sidney S. Ford and "a man named Bailey," did not reach the actual summit, they suggest he at least reached the crater rim – a remarkable achievement for its time. Another daring party, led by Lieutenant August V. Kautz in 1857, managed to ascend to above 12,000 feet via the Kautz Glacier, reaching a high point near the summit plateau, but not reaching the summit due to high winds, poor snow conditions and impending darkness.

The Stars and Stripes adorn Columbia Crest. (Photo: National Park Service)

On August 17, 1870, Philemon Van Trump and Hazard Stevens reached the summit and claimed the first ascent. Their guide, Sluiskin, led them in a roundabout fashion to very near what is now Paradise, where the pair ascended past present-day Camp Muir and along Gibraltar Ledge to the summit crater, despite Sluiskin's warnings that they would be swept off the mountain "like a withered leaf." Darkness descended on the summit, and they endured a night in the summit steam (firn) caves before descending. Sluiskin believed they had died on the summit. When the pair returned to their camp the next day, the Indian thought their ghosts were returning to haunt him for predicting their demise.

A handful of ascents were made prior to the turn of the century, including an ascent in October 1870 by Samuel Emmons and A.D. Wilson, via the Emmons Glacier. In 1883, Van Trump led George Bayle and James Longmire to the summit. John Muir climbed Mount Rainier in 1888, along with A.C. Warner, who took the first photographs from the summit. Fay Fuller, the first woman to reach the summit, made her ascent in 1890. In 1897, the Mazamas club from Portland, Oregon brought over 200 members to Mount Rainier, of which 58 were successful in reaching the summit. Among them was Professor Edgar McClure, who became the first known climbing fatality on Mount Rainier when he fell while descending from a rock above Paradise (now McClure Rock).

After his 1883 ascent of Mount Rainier, during which he discovered and named Longmire Springs, James Longmire returned to settle near present-day Longmire. In 1884, Longmire opened the Mineral Spring Resort, a moderately successful venture that exploited the mineral springs. In 1890, Longmire began the first road to Longmire Springs, and five years later opened the first trail to Paradise Valley. Longmire is the park's oldest developed area. The present-day National Park Inn is open for guests year-round. Visitors can see remnants of the Longmire settlement by walking the Trail of the Shadows.

Early visitors to Paradise hiked up crude trails from Longmire. After 1895, Paradise became more popular as a tourist destination. It now is the most-visited area of the park, having abundant visitor services, trails, views and winter recreation opportunities. In 1911, an automobile reached Paradise, and later that year President

Old-time travellers motor up the Paradise Highway.
(Photo: National Park Service)

William Howard Taft made the journey. Hardy visitors can hike remnants of the old trail from Longmire to Paradise, although most are content to drive there. Paradise Inn was constructed in 1917, burned down many years later, and was rebuilt in its present form.

Models (circa 1920) pose in the latest swimwear on Nisqually Glacier. (Photo: National Park Service)

Human travel on Mount Rainier began along animal trails leading to meadows and other feeding grounds. These trails were altered little by native hunters who ventured onto the mountain's high ridges in pursuit of deer and mountain goat. Homesteaders and tourists eventually "improved" trails through increased use and construction, until crudely-constructed trails reached several favorite destinations, including Paradise and other high meadows around the mountain. In 1915, The Mountaineers made an en masse circumnavigation of Mount Rainier, an enterprise that took several weeks of packing around the mountain, exploring the high meadows and forested valleys, and a summit climb via the Emmons-Winthrop Glacier. Other around-the-mountain trips followed, although these were slowed greatly by the lack of established trails in many areas. In the 1930s, the Civilian Conservation Corps built many of the trails that are in use today, including the Wonderland Trail.

Mount Rainier National Park

The uniqueness and grandeur of Mount Rainier and its surrounding forest and parkland was recognized early enough that the area was preserved by the establishment of the National Park on March 2, 1899. Despite the threat imposed by the sleeping giant, Mount Rainier remains one of the most popular of America's national parks. It is visited by millions annually; these tourists mostly crowd its narrow, winding roads, visitor centers and interpretive trails. Fewer visitors venture into the pristine wilderness areas surrounding the mountain. Fewer still are those who come to climb the mountain, of which about half are successful.

More immediate than the threat of volcanic eruption is the threat of human misuse, overuse and abuse to the park's wild areas. Visitors to Mount Rainier National Park should keep in mind that much of the park is wilderness and requires special care. Although the mountain appears rugged and indestructible, its fragile meadows and virgin forests can be devastated by careless use. To minimize human impacts on the park's varied ecosystems, and to maintain the spirit of conservancy stated in the National Park Organic Act of 1916 ("to conserve the scenery and the natural and historic objects and the wildlife therein and to provide for the enjoyment of the same in such manner and by such means as will leave them unimpaired for the enjoyment of future generations"), a

Wilderness Management Plan has been adopted, limiting the kinds and frequency of use the park's wilderness areas.

Park Service Regulations

The Park Service has adopted a number of rules for use of Mount Rainier National Park, some of which are listed here. All Park Service rules and regulations contained here and elsewhere in this guide are current as of May 1998, but are subject to change without notice. For current regulations, contact the Park Service or check the Mount Rainier National Park homepage, **www.nps.gov/mora/**.

• Between June 1 and September 30, backpackers must obtain a permit and pay a $10.00 wilderness permit fee, plus $5.00 for each person in the party. The permit is good for up to 14 days. No permit or fee is required for day hiking. Permits may be obtained from Longmire and White River Hiker Information Centers, as well as Paradise, Carbon River, Ohanapecosh and Sunrise ranger stations. Call the Backcountry Desk at (360) 569-2211 for information. A "backcountry trip planner" is available upon request. THERE IS NO LONGER ANY SELF-REGISTRATION – YOU MUST GET YOUR PERMIT FROM A PARK RANGER!

• Visitors intending to go above Camp Muir or Camp Schurman, or to travel on glaciers, must fill out a climber registration card prior to the climb (a $15.00 fee or $25.00 annual pass).

• Camping party sizes are limited. Specific party size limits for different zones are contained where relevant in the following chapters.

• Camping on vegetation is not permitted in the Alpine Zone (and is discouraged elsewhere within the park).

• No pets (except guide dogs) are permitted on trails or within the backcountry or wilderness areas, except on the Pacific Crest Trail. On the PCT, pets must be restrained, and not permitted to run loose.

• Visitors must pack out their trash.

• Fires are not permitted anywhere within the wilderness or backcountry.

• Firearms and weapons of any kind are prohibited within the park, unless packed away and unloaded.

Although climbing and scrambling are acceptable pursuits in Mount Rainier National Park, be aware that some forms of outdoor adventure are strictly illegal, including hang gliding, parapenting, and wilderness mountain biking. Also, solo climbing requires advance written permission from the park superintendent.

By following the above rules and others contained in this guide, and by using common sense, you can help ensure that the wild areas of Mount Rainier National Park will endure for future visitors. Most visitors assume the park has been reserved for their pleasure. In reality, the park was set aside to preserve the integrity of the wilderness for all of us, if for no other reason than so we can remember what reality looks like. Do your best to keep it intact for those who will come after you are gone.

"No-Trace Ethic"

Backcountry use at Mount Rainier National Park is on the rise again, and along with this increase is an increase in overuse and abuse of many fragile areas of the park. The Park Service recommends that visitors to the Wilderness areas of Mount Rainier adopt the "no-trace" ethic, by adhering to the guidelines that follow.

- Travel in small groups to do less damage to meadows and campsites.
- Use a stove for cooking, and bring a tent or shelter.
- Use pit toilets or use accepted human waste disposal practices (such as not eliminating near water sources, and burying your waste in organic material, or packing it out).
- Plan your actions so as to make the least impact on the environment.
- Stay on trails, even when muddy, to avoid sidecutting or erosion, and don't take shortcuts on switchbacks, which leads to considerable erosion, and can be dangerous to you and those below you.
- Choose stable sites for camps and rest stops, rather than on fragile vegetation.
- Avoid having leftover food, so as not to attract wildlife to your camp.

Other impact-minimizing techniques are included in this guide where they will have the most relevance.

The many people who visit Mount Rainier must remember there is only one Mount Rainier. To preserve it for the future, we must treat it with care and respect. Remember the old motto, "Take only pictures, leave only footprints," – just be careful not to leave your footprints where they will do irreparable damage.

Western red cedars tower above in the Grove of the Patriarchs. (Photo: National Park Service)

Chapter Two:
Flora and Fauna

Although few visitors come specifically to seek out species of plants and animals, with the exception of photographers and wildflower enthusiasts, the park's abundant plant and animal life is an integral part of the Mount Rainier experience. Learning to recognize plants and animals in their native environment is not easy, but is very rewarding.

Flora

The plant life of Mount Rainier National Park is varied and abundant. The lowland forests are occupied by giants: old-growth Douglas fir, western hemlock and western red cedar. In their shade grow a variety of other plants, including mushrooms, mosses and ferns. The larger trees are replaced by Pacific silver fir and noble fir as one ascends the mountain's slopes. Wildflowers begin to appear along with underbrush, including huckleberry and blueberry. As one climbs higher, the "silver fir forest" is replaced with other trees: mountain hemlock, Alaska yellow cedar, subalpine fir. Englemann spruce and lodgepole pine make rare appearances in the Sunrise area, and whitebark pine grows on the mountain's eastern flanks. At higher, exposed elevations, trees cluster together in dense "islands," which offer protection from the wind and snow of higher elevation. Low shrubs of huckleberry and heather compliment the wide-open meadows of grasses and wildflowers, including splendid blooms of avalanche lillies and Indian paintbrush. Above treeline, trees thin out, leaving isolated islands of gnarled and dwarfed krummholz. Heather grows wherever there is shelter from the wind, and a few hardy flower species cling to the barren, windswept soil. Higher yet, among the snow and ice of the mountain, tiny lichens eke out a meager existence on sunny rocks, and pinkish algae thrives in stagnant snow.

Obviously, this is a simplistic overview of park plant life and ecosystems. There are so many species of plants within the park (more than 75 species of wildflowers in the sub-alpine meadows alone have been identified) that, to name them all here, let alone describe them in any detail, would leave little room in this book for anything else. Whole volumes have been produced documenting the plant life of Mount Rainier and the surrounding Cascade Range. However, as a practical matter, the typical park visitor isn't interested in the minutiae of minor subspecies of moss and lichen, nor will he or she likely be inclined to spend much time seeking out specific plant species. Visitors interested in identifying plants within Mount Rainier National Park should consult the bibliography for topic-specific references and expect to spend a great deal of time scrutinizing selected areas of the park.

Wildflowers are the most sought-after plants in the park. The best times for viewing many of the park's wildflowers are late July and early August, when the park's high meadows are awash in colorful blossoms. Tourists and nature hikers will find wildflowers abundant at Paradise and Sunrise after June; summertime backcountry travelers will assuredly be rewarded by immense, blooming meadows. DON'T PICK WILDFLOWERS! Not only is flower picking damaging to the beauty of the park, it is illegal to molest any park plants or animals; you may be cited for the offense.

In contrast to the wide-openness of the park's many high meadows, the old-growth forests are equally important and impressive. One-thousand-year-old stands of Douglas fir, western red cedar and other timber giants loom among the lower elevations of the park, particularly in the Nisqually, Ohanapecosh, White and Carbon river valleys. The contrast between the replanted Douglas fir forests outside the park and the virgin forests within the park is very striking and will make a lasting impression.

Several species of plants that reside only in Mount Rainier National Park are struggling for survival; one careless footstep could bring extinction. Follow the Park Service's motto: "Don't be a meadow stomper!"

Fauna

It is likely that, on certain summer weekends, man is the most abundant species of animal found in Mount Rainier National Park, with the exception of the many birds, rodents and insects residing here. However, numerous other animals make Mount Rainier and its surrounding woodlands their home. Yellow pine chipmunks and golden-mantled ground squirrels are the small, easily identifiable rodents you surely will see scampering about on roads, trails, campgrounds and in picnic areas throughout the park. Hoary marmots, the "groundhogs of the west," are abundant throughout rocky areas of the sub-alpine zone, (along with occasional populations of Yellowbelly marmots, say some observers, although officially there are no Yellowbellies here). The marmot's shrill whistle is easily recognizable, and they frequently can be seen scurrying through the talus. The pika (say "pee-ka" to pronounce it correctly, although "pie-ka" is more common), another rodent-like creature (actually of the rabbit family), is more elusive than the marmot. These guinea-pig sized creatures have a very shrill "eek," and resemble large mice, but without a visible tail. Where you find marmots, you likely will find pika.

Porcupines sometimes are seen within the park. They are easy to identify by their quills. They live on tree bark, leaves and branches, like the beaver, although they climb trees instead of cutting them down. While humans rarely need worry about porcupine encounters, dogs and other attackers frequently are impaled by the porcupine's quills, which sink deeper into flesh with attempts to extract them. The only problem porcupines may cause humans has to do with food: Porcupines crave salt and fat, and will eat just about anything containing fat and salt to get it, including your boots, backpack, clothing, and even certain auto parts, like tires, belts and hoses. Sleep close to your boots and pack if you see a porcupine near your camp!

Beavers are seen rarely within the park, although their work may be observed readily along Trail of the Shadows, below Tahoma Vista picnic area, and near Chenuis Falls trailhead. If you can't find a live beaver in Longmire Meadows, there is a stuffed beaver at Longmire Museum. The snowshoe hare, another scarce creature, is the park's only native species of rabbit (except the pika, which most everybody assumes is a rodent). It is found throughout the park, but rarely is seen. Although they inhabit the park year around, all you're likely to see of these timid creatures is their distinctive tracks in new-fallen snow.

One of the more frequently observed park animals is the black-tailed deer. Park deer commonly dwell below treeline, and are usually found in forest and meadow areas throughout the park. Elk, the largest of Mount Rainier's mammals, roam in herds in the high meadows and subalpine forests of the park. In September, the male elk's mating call can often be heard in the eastern portion of the park. Mountain goats, another of the park's abundant residents, roam the high ridges, meadows and crags throughout most of the park, staying near snowline all year round. Mountain goats frequently are seen in the early morning and late evening, when they descend to alpine meadows for feeding. In early season, their coats may appear dirty and ragged, but by late season, after shedding their winter coat, the take on their characteristic pure white color.

Don't Feed The Bears!

Black bears live in Mount Rainier National Park. They are seen most often at campground garbage sites and wherever there is food, especially huckleberries and blueberries. Visitors rarely encounter bears, since the bears are afraid of humans, and usually go out of their way to avoid them. If you encounter a bear, keep your distance. Don't feed the bears, not only for your own safety but because bears can become dependent upon handouts. Bear attacks are very rare, but some "problem bears" become agressive when in pursuit of food. If you encounter a bear, remember that they are usually near-sighted and may want to get closer to see what you are and whether you pose a threat. If the bear charges, keep still and don't run away, as that may anger the

bear. If the bear still comes after you, remain still and, as a last resort, play dead. This is not a guarantee that the bear will leave you alone, but is recommended by most authorities as the best strategy.

Bears don't like humans, but they do like human food and will do extraordinary things to get it. Defensive strategies are best for avoiding bear encounters. When camping, put your food where bears can't get at it. Don't leave food scraps out, and don't cook more than you will eat. It is a good idea to do your cooking and cleaning well away from your tent, and to leave all food, garbage and anything with an aroma of food or garbage, including the clothes you wore while cooking, at this site. Hanging your food and garbage well off the ground (the general rule is

A brown bear scavenges food from trash left by park visitors. (Photo: National Park Service)

10 feet up and 5 feet away from tree trunks) and well away from your tent, even when going off on short trips, is recommended. The Park Service suggests bringing a bear-resistant food container, since suitable trees aren't always available. Don't leave food unattended at your camp or in your pack, even for a few minutes. Whatever you do, don't use your food bag as a pillow! If a bear approaches your campsite, make loud noises (bang pots and pans, blow a whistle, etc.) to frighten it away. Don't be too aggressive, though, since bears often respond aggressively if they feel threatened. If the bear doesn't run off after all this, you have a problem. Don't get between a problem bear and food. Also, stay away from bear cubs if you know what's good for you!

Cougars, or mountain lions, also inhabit the forests of Mount Rainier National Park. Cougars have become an increasing threat to humans in western states during the past several years. Whild attacks on people are still rare, cougars sightings are up. Cougars tend to stalk and attack solitary prey, usually deer and small game, but do occasionally attack humans, In one notable case in Montana, a cougar killed a young boy who had run ahead on the trail during a family hike. Cougars have been known to stalk solo hikers for miles, and to attack trail runners. Although there have been no reported cougar attacks at Mount Rainier during recent years, you should be wary of cougars just the same. Don't hike alone, especially in remote areas. Keep your party together, especially if you have children with you. If you encounter a cougar that doesn't immediately run away, maintain eye contact as you back away slowly; don't turn and run, as this seems to trigger a chase instinct in cats. Don't worry too much; you probably won't even see a cougar track, let alone an actual cougar. But then again, you just might, so be prepared.

More than 120 different species of birds reside within the park (too many to name here). Insects and other "lower" life forms will not even be discussed in this book, except to say they are abundant (especially mosquitos and deer flies) and provide an important food source for many of the park's birds and small mammals.

A few varieties of fish reside in the park's lakes and streams, including cutthroat, rainbow and brook trout. Most fish are survivors of past stocking, and exotic (not native) species may be removed in the future. Fishing is permitted in most areas of the park; check with the Park Service about current regulations. Fishermen intent upon a big catch may be disappointed in Mount Rainier National Park, as there are few fish, and even fewer of these are ever caught.

When encountering park animals in the backcountry, keep your distance, for yours and the animal's safety. Hunting, trapping or otherwise molesting, injuring or disturbing park animals and birds is strictly prohibited (except for fish, subject to the current regulations). When viewing animals from your car, please pull off the road so you are out of the way of other motorists. Also, don't get out of your car to feed any park animals, particularly bears, which can be very unpredictable and dangerous.

You should not feed any park animals. They can become dependent upon human handouts, which makes life difficult for them during the off-season, especially for squirrels, chipmunks, raccoons and bears. The park's limited natural food supply is sufficient to sustain abundant populations of park animals without your "help."

Granted, this is a very sparse overview of park wildlife, but it would take an entire separate volume to properly describe and identify all park animals. If you are interested in learning more about park animals, there are many topic-specific books and other resources available.

Chapter Three:
Auto and Bicycle Touring

Most visitors are introduced to the wonders of Mount Rainier National Park from the comfort of their automobiles. Most scarcely get out of their cars, in fact, and then only to look at the visitor center exhibits or to use the restroom. Others choose to view the scenery from the saddles of their bicycles. The roads of Mount Rainier National Park, which accomodate both autos and bicycles, are described briefly in this guide. However, this is not a car-touring nor a bicycle-touring guide, but one focusing on wilderness use. Those interested only in motor touring can do pretty well with a Washington State highway roadmap, which contains a detail map of the park and its roads.

Park roads, trails and visitor services are used heavily on sunny summer weekends. If you want to avoid the crowds, come during the week when the park is comparatively empty. Call ahead in spring and early summer to check road conditions; flooding often prompts road closures until repair work can be completed in July.

Access Fees and Permits

Park entry fees are required at all entry stations (Nisqually, Stevens Canyon, White River, Carbon River) – unless you arrive late or early enough, while the entrance station is closed. There is no entry fee at Mowich Lake, or for travel on Highway 410 or State Route 123. Entry fees are presently:

$5 for single person entry by foot, bicycle, bus passengers or motorcycle (valid 7 days; persons 16 and under enter free)
$10.00 for single vehicle entry (valid for 7 days)
$20.00 for Mount Rainier National Park one-year pass (valid for one year from month of purchase)
$10.00 for Golden Age Passport (lifetime pass for U.S. residents 62 years and older, valid at all federal fee areas)
$50.00 for Golden Eagle Passport (valid at all federal entrance fee parks for one year from month of purchase)
Free Golden Access Passport (lifetime pass for U.S. citizens or permanent residents who are blind or permanently disabled)

Other fees include:

Auto camping fees of $10.00-$14.00 per night. Reservations are required for Ohanapecosh and Cougar Rock campgrounds between July 1 and Labor Day; otherwise, campgrounds are available on a first-come, first-served basis. To make reservations, call 1-800-365-CAMP (2267), fax 1-301-722-1174, or write to National Park Reservation Service, P.O. Box 1600, Cumberland MD 21502.

A new Wilderness Permit Fee program is in effect as of 1998. from June 1 through September 30, backpackers must obtain a wilderness permit and pay a $10.00 fee, plus $5.00 for each person in the party (regardless of age). The permit is valid for up to 14 days. An annual permit is available at a cost of $40.00 per person. No permit is required for day hikers, other than the park entry fee.

A climbing permit fee of $15.00 is required to climb Mount Rainier. An annual pass i available for $25.00 for those who plan on climbing the mountain or venturing onto the glaciers more than once per season.

Park visitors 16 years or under, or 62 years or older are not charged an admission fee. Visitors 62 years or older may obtain a free Golden Age Passport, which entitles them to unlimited access to the park and reduced-rate camping for one year. Golden Access Passports are available free to disabled visitors from the Park Service administrative offices. School groups may obtain a waiver of the entry fee if they are on a nature study field trip and make a prior written request, on school stationery, to the Park Service administrative office. Frequent park visitors should consider investing $15 in an annual pass, which is available at the entrance station or by mail from Park Service administrative offices. A $25 annual pass is available, which entitles the holder to unlimited access to all United States National Parks for one calendar year.

Theft and Vandalism

Vandalism and theft are not everyday occurences in Mount Rainier National Park, but they do happen. You can do much to minimize your risk of theft, including parking at heavy-use and high-visibility trailheads, locking all valuables in the trunk of your car, not leaving anything visible inside your car, taking your keys and wallet with you, and not leaving notes or telling strangers where you've gone or when you'll be back. Theives usually go for high-priced items, so if you leave your camera and a bunch of climbing equipment visible in your car, you may find it gone when you return. Car theft, while rare, does happen occasionally. Report suspicious persons loitering near trailheads and parking areas to a park ranger. Vandalism is a bit harder to avoid. Parking in high-use, high-visibility areas is the best deterrent. Most often, windows are broken to give access to would-be thieves. Sometimes, though, vandalism is random and wanton. Report all criminal activity to the nearest park ranger, or to park headquarters by calling (360) 569-2211, or dial 911.

Bicycling at Mount Rainier

Bicycle touring around Mount Rainier has become more popular in recent years. Although the roads are steep and obviously not intended for bicycle use (narrow shoulders, steep grades, numerous curves, much traffic), they are very scenic and challenging. If you want to bicycle in the park, come during the week, when auto traffic will not be as heavy. And make sure your brakes work before you come!

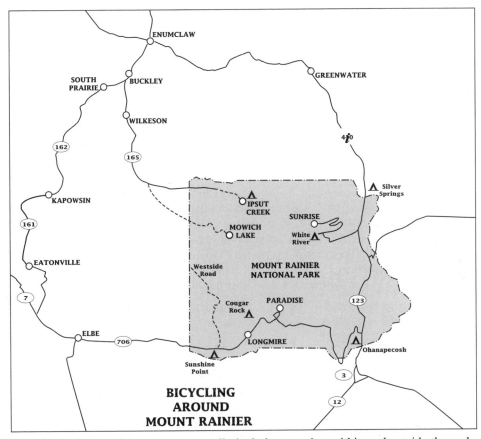

BICYCLING AROUND MOUNT RAINIER

Bicycle touring at a leisurely pace usually includes camping within and outside the park. The usual loop route begins from Enumclaw and wraps counterclockwise around the mountain, with overnight stops at Cougar Rock, Ohanapecosh and White River or Silver Springs Campgrounds before the final descent to Enumclaw.

Mountain bikes are permitted on park roads, subject to the usual traffic and bicycle regulations, but the Park Service forbids their presence on all trails. Westside Road is an enjoyable mountain bike route without auto traffic; when flood damaged, it sometimes is open to cyclists. Hikers and climbers often use mountain bikes to access Westside Road trailheads. Bicycles are not permitted in wilderness areas of the park, which soon may include Westside Road. When Westside Road is open for autos, cyclists must stop where the road ends near Klapatche Point. Unless otherwise stated by the Park Service, any "closed" road inside Mount Rainier National Park, whether paved or not, is off limits to cyclists.

Preparation for an around-the-mountain bicycle tour should include much hill work, as there are many uphill miles. Be prepared for any weather conditions, from hot and sunny to cold and rainy or snow. Rain can mean hypothermia to an unprepared rider – a rain and windproof shell is a must. Bring plenty of water on your ride, and drink often to avoid dehydration.

Although most cyclists take three days or more to tour the mountain, there is an annual organized ride that invites riders to circle the mountain in a single day. This "Ride Around Mount Rainier in One Day" (R.A.M.R.O.D.) is a brutal test of endurance, with 154 miles of riding and over 10,000 feet of elevation gain on the park's steep, narrow roads. Those who want to enjoy the scenery should take their time. Park regulations limit the number of cyclists who may enter the park on a given day, so it is best to check with park rangers prior to riding into the park. Ordinarily, it is not a problem, as R.A.M.R.O.D. has been moved to a weekday, but if you choose to tour the park the same day as R.A.M.R.O.D., forget it! (Anyone interested in participating in R.A.M.R.O.D. should write to 2814 N.E. 177th Place, Seattle, WA 98155 for information.)

Paradise Highway – State Route 706

Although it is not the most scenic road in Mount Rainier National Park (that honor going to the road to Sunrise, in the author's estimation), the Paradise Highway certainly is the most popular. More than twice as many people visit Paradise than Sunrise or any other destination within the park, mostly because the Paradise Highway is open year-round, while other roads within the park are usually closed from early winter through early summer – and also because it is easily accessible from Puget Sound and offers more tourist accomodations and attractions than other destinations within the park.

A good history of the Paradise Highway, from its early days as an Indian trail to being paved in concrete, is found in *Highway To Paradise* (Nadeau, Valley Press 1983).

For most visitors, the journey to Paradise begins via State Route 7, which is followed south from Tacoma along approximately the original "Highway to Paradise." The journey also can begin on U.S. 12 from I-5 just south of Centralia/Chehalis. State Route 706 leads east from Elbe through Ashford, past park headquarters and several motels and restaurants, to the Nisqually Entrance.

The road curves up and up, with stunning views of Mount Rainier and the Nisqually Glacier. The visitor center is just ahead on the left, and the main parking lot and ranger

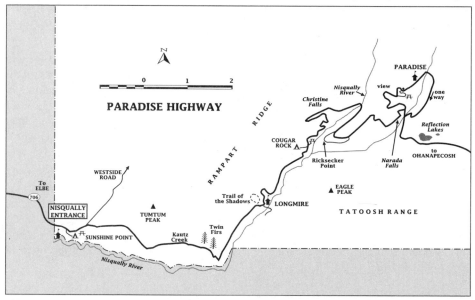

station shortly beyond. On busy weekends, you'd sooner find a parking space at a shopping mall than at Paradise. Paradise was named by Mrs. Eclain Longmire on her first visit to the area in 1885. Unfortunately, these days, it little resembles the "heavenly paradise" she beheld over a century ago.

Westside Road

The Westside Road forks northward up Tahoma Creek beginning about one mile (1½ km) inside the Nisqually Entrance. This gravel road is probably more bumpy than the majority of park visitors would like. The road has been washed out by debris flows and floods at several places in the first several miles along Tahoma Creek, and flood warnings are posted along the way. Most travel Westside Road only to access trails. From the park boundary near Klapatche Point, the road is limited to foot and stock travel only.

Westside Road usually is closed til mid-July. Access frequently is limited due to repairs of flood damage. Westside Road was closed for all of 1990 due to flood damage, and the Park Service planned to make repairs (again!) during 1991, closing the road beyond Dry Creek. Depending on the availability of funding and the financial viability of continual repairs, it may well be closed perm-anently. Check current road conditions when you enter the park, or call ahead.

Mowich Lake – State Route 165

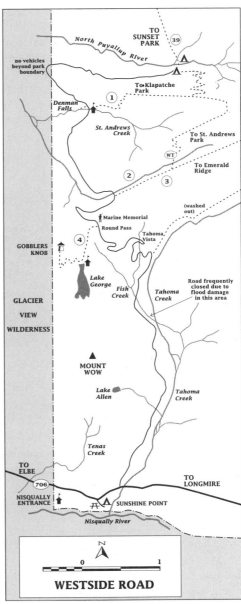

WESTSIDE ROAD

State Route 165 leads through Wilkeson and Carbonado, and the clearcut Carbon River Valley, before it becomes a prominently marked, unpaved righthand fork off the paved Carbon River Road, which continues east to the Carbon River Entrance. The road ascends uneventfully but bumpily through unbroken replanted forest to the park boundary, then breaks into wide-open old growth forest as it climbs toward Mowich Lake. In winter, the road usually is snowbound from the park boundary, where it is gated until snow free.

Call ahead if you intend to start your overnight trip from Mowich Lake; if you can't get a permit there, you'll have to go to Carbon River Entrance. A walk-in campground is located at the southeast end of the parking area, and is available on a first-comers' basis (permits may be required). Backcountry permits may be obtained from the USFS White River Ranger District office in Enumclaw if you are entering the park via Forest Service land or in winter (if self-registration in winter is discontinued); call first to make sure (253) 825-6585. Permits are issued from Mowich Lake on weekends only from July through mid-September; otherwise, you must get them from Carbon River.

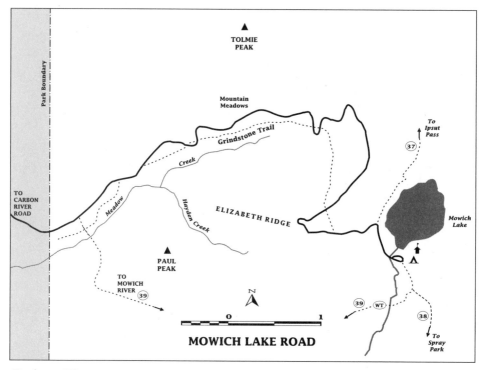

MOWICH LAKE ROAD

Carbon River

The Carbon River Entrance is reached easily by continuing on the paved Carbon River Road south of Carbonado from the point where Route 165 forks southward towards Mowich Lake. There is a ranger station at the entrance, and a self-guided nature trail looping through the only known inland temperate rain forest in North America. Backcountry permits and climbing cards may be obtained at the entrance station when it is open. During winter, Backcountry permits may be obtained from the USFS White River Ranger District office in Enumclaw (call (253) 825-6585 for details).

Carbon River Road is closed during the winter from the park boundary, making it accessible only to hikers, skiers and snowshoers, depending upon winter snow conditions. Call ahead if you want to visit Ipsut Creek during the winter months to check road conditions and accessibility, and permit availability. Road damage frequently limits vehicle access to this area. Call ahead to check on current road conditions before planning a trip to Carbon River.

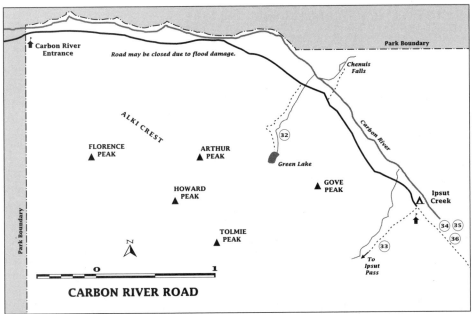

CARBON RIVER ROAD

Mather Memorial Highway
U.S. Highway 410

The Mather Memorial Highway enters the park from the north (from Enumclaw) and the east (from Yakima), crossing Chinook Pass. For those arriving from Enumclaw, the White River Road turnoff is the most notable feature. At Cayuse Pass the highway veers east, and in two tight switchbacks ascends to Tipsoo Lake and Chinook Pass.

Highway 410 is closed during the winter from the park boundary. Check road accessibility in advance of your trip from October through June. Highway 410 is a high-maintenance highway, which is frequently under repair. Be prepared for delays or closures, particularly during summer weekdays. Call the Park Service at (360) 569-2211 to check on current road conditions.

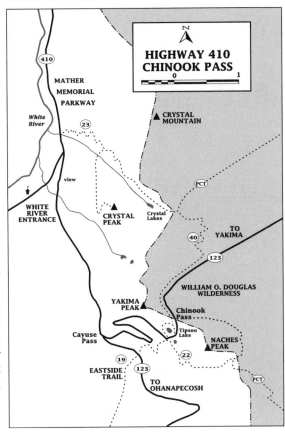

White River and Sunrise Road

About four miles from the northern entrance of the park, the White River Road forks off conspicuously from Highway 410, heading west towards Mount Rainier – which for those entering from Enumclaw has remained almost invisible to this point. After one mile, the entrance ranger station is reached. Climbers and overnight hikers must register and obtain permits here, or at Sunrise Ranger Station when it is open. The road continues to a well-marked side road forking left to White River Campground.

White River entrance and campground are closed during the winter, and usually are open by July each year.

The White River Road continues from the entrance to White River Campground another ten spectacular miles to Sunrise, the most-scenic and second-most-popular destination in the park. This road sometimes is open by Memorial Day, but can open as late as July. The Sunrise Road, highest in the park and the highest paved road in Washington State, is usually closed sometime in October each year, soon after the season's first snowfall.

The ascent to Sunrise is one of the finest motor tours in the western United States, and is a must for any first-time park visitor. If the climb through the forest zones was not enough to make it worthwhile, the views are! The road hugs the steep mountainside without guard rails, making this a memorable if not unnerving drive for squeamish passengers. The road levels out after Sunrise Point for a scenic three miles through the

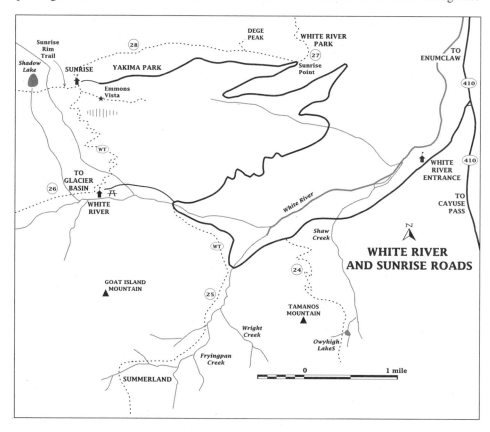

wide-open expanses of Yakima Park before reaching Sunrise (elevation 6,400 ft.). Like Paradise, Sunrise has abundant visitor services. Also like Paradise, off-trail hiking is a citable offense. Please stay on the trails here, as plant communities are having a hard enough time surviving in this bleak environment without being trampled under-foot.

The road to Sunrise is closed during the winter, usually immediately following the season's first snowfall in October. It sometimes is reopened as early as Memorial Day, but you should call ahead to ask about road conditions if you want to visit Sunrise before July.

Ohanapecosh – Highway 123

Visitors entering the park from the south via State Route 123 will pass Ohanapecosh Campground within a mile of the park boundary. Ohanapecosh is the largest campground within the park, with 232 campsites and full facilities. Another two miles north from the campground is the Stevens Canyon Entrance turnoff and entrance station. The highway follows the Ohanapecosh River and Chinook Creek toward Cayuse Pass to meet U.S. Highway 410.

Ohanapecosh Campground usually is accessible year round, but the highway beyond is closed during winter months, sometimes not opening until July. Reservations are required for Ohanapecosh Campground from July 1 through Labor Day; call 1-800-365-CAMP (2267) to make reservations.

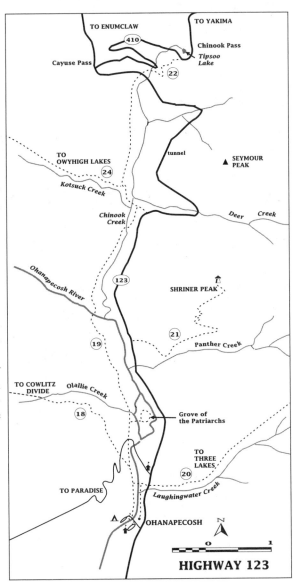

Stevens Canyon

The turnoff to Stevens Canyon Entrance from State Route 123 is about 2½ miles inside the park from the south boundary. The road is closed during winter months, and usually opens before July. Flood damage repairs sometimes delay the opening of Stevens Canyon Road until late summer. The road climbs over Backbone Ridge to Box Canyon, then continues for several miles through Stevens Canyon, passing several frightening rock outcroppings and overhangs. After some hairpin curves, the road passes Reflection Lakes and curves past Inspiration Point to meet the Paradise Highway.

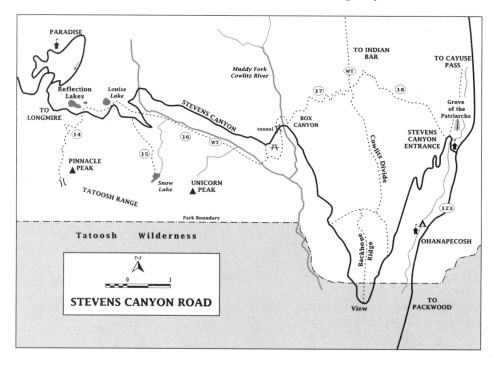

Chapter Four:
Hiking Trails

Hiking the trails of Mount Rainier National Park is the most popular way of becoming acquainted with the mountain and its surrounding forest and parkland. There are more than 300 miles of maintained trails within the park: short and long hikes to lakes, treks through glacial valleys and flower-blanketed meadows and climbs to mountaintops, all of which offer close-up views of the park's flora, fauna and many geological landmarks. There are hikes within the park to match the ambitions of any who want to experience the park up close.

You should visit one of the Hiker Information Centers before going on any backcountry trip. Hiker Information Centers are located at Longmire and White River Ranger Stations. The centers contain maps and other information to help you plan your stay. Rangers on duty will provide you with the necessary permits, current trail information and Park Service Wilderness-use regulations. It is a good idea to check trail conditions before any hike. Bridges are sometimes washed out, and the ranger can give you an up-to-date trail report. Overnight visitors must obtain a permit before venturing into the wilderness. Backcountry permits may be obtained from Hiker Information Centers, as well as Carbon River, Ohanapecosh, Nisqually Entrance, Sunrise, Paradise and Wilkeson ranger stations, and sometimes at Mowich Lake on weekends between July and mid-September (if you can find the ranger). Backpackers leaving from Mowich Lake must get their permits from the Carbon River ranger station when not available at Mowich Lake. Those entering the park

A hiker follows the trail from Sunrise to Second Burroughs Mountain. (Photo: Arvel Gentry)

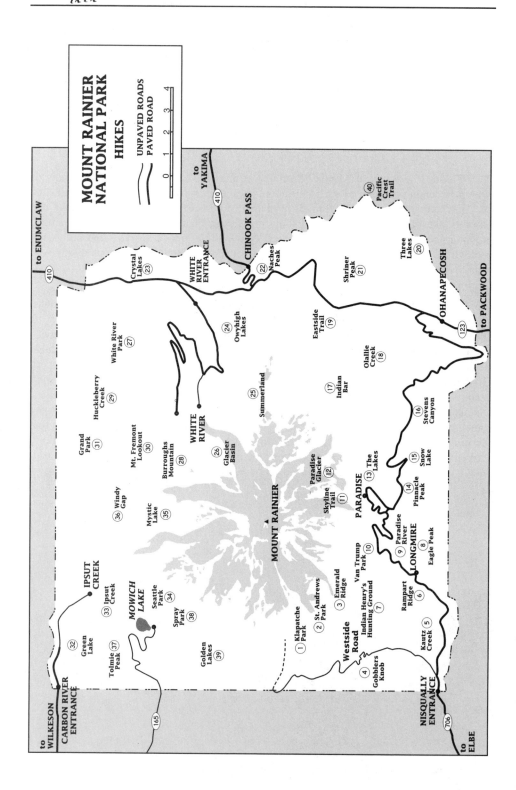

MOUNT RAINIER
NATIONAL PARK

HIKES

UNPAVED ROADS
PAVED ROAD

0 1 2 3 4

to ENUMCLAW

to YAKIMA

CHINOOK PASS

410

40 Pacific Crest Trail

22 Naches Peak

Crystal Lakes 23

WHITE RIVER ENTRANCE

Shriner Peak 21

Three Lakes 20

OHANAPECOSH

to PACKWOOD

123

24 Owyhigh Lakes

Eastside Trail 19

White River Park 27

Olallie Creek 18

Huckleberry Creek 29

17 Indian Bar

Summerland 25

16 Stevens Canyon

Grand Park 31

Mt. Fremont Lookout 30

Burroughs Mountain 28

WHITE RIVER

Glacier Basin 26

Paradise Glacier 12

15 Snow Lake

13 The Lakes

14 Pinnacle Peak

MOUNT RAINIER

Skyline Trail 11

PARADISE

Windy Gap 36

Mystic Lake 35

Paradise River 10

9 Eagle Peak

8 Eagle Peak

LONGMIRE

IPSUT CREEK

Ipsut Creek

Seattle Park 34

Van Trump Park 10

Rampart Ridge 6

Green Lake 32

Tolmie Peak 37

33 Ipsut Creek

MOWICH LAKE

Spray Park 38

Emerald Ridge 3

Indian Henry's Hunting Ground 7

Kautz Creek 5

CARBON RIVER ENTRANCE

to WILKESON

Golden Lakes 39

1 Klapatche Park

2 St. Andrews Park

Westside Road

4 Gobblers Knob

NISQUALLY ENTRANCE

165

706

to ELBE

via Forest Service lands may obtain permits from the White River Ranger District office in Enumclaw.

Trails in this guide will be graded with the following symbols to denote the difficulty and length of the hike:

● These hikes are not long nor very strenuous, and will take no longer than a few hours, round trip. Suitable for hikers of all ages. Bring water and a snack, and raingear.

■ These hikes may involve several miles of moderately strenuous hiking, and may take half a day to a full day, round trip. Bring hiking boots, raingear, water and lunch. Be prepared for changing weather. Some parties will camp overnight, but more often by choice rather than out of necessity.

▲ These hikes are longer and more strenuous, taking a day or more to travel round trip. Many of these hikes can be done in a day by strong hikers moving fast, but most will spend at least one night in the backcountry. Bring hiking boots, raingear, water, lunch, and extra food and clothing, and overnight gear if camping.

Distances of hikes will be provided in miles and kilometers, and an estimated hiking time is provided. All distances are approximate. Hiking times will vary, but the estimated time assumes you are walking at a moderate, steady pace (two miles per hour average), with an allowance for rest stops. Elevation gain figures are rounded off, and include all elevation gained on the entire hike; on round trip and loop hikes, there will be a corresponding loss of elevation.

Routes marked with (12) are hiking trails

When camping in the wilderness areas of Mount Rainier National Park, try to minimize your impact:

- Use established campsites.
- Don't camp on vegetation.
- Don't create new campsites.
- Don't cut down trees to make shelters; bring a tent instead.
- Use stoves; no fires are allowed.
- Leave pets at home; they are not allowed in the backcountry.
- Bring a collapsible water bucket to reduce the number of trips you must make for water.

Be conscientious when you hike in Mount Rainier's wilderness areas:

- Stay on trails.
- Don't cut switchbacks.
- Don't leave anything behind.
- Make sure you put out your cigarettes before moving on (better yet, don't smoke!).
- Clean up after yourself. Your mother doesn't live in Mount Rainier's wilderness areas, and Mother Nature isn't likely to clean up after you – but watch out if she does!

When you are issued a permit, you must follow your itinerary exactly. If you change your plans and decide to camp somewhere other than the location stated on your permit, you must get a new permit from a wilderness ranger. If you camp somewhere other than where you planned, you could be cited. Be polite to park rangers even if they are about to give you a citation, because they might just give you a warning instead. If you are rude or defensive, you can pretty much count on being fined.

Backcountry Camping Regulations

As a part of its Wilderness Management Plan, the Park Service has adopted the following rules regarding backcountry camping:

• A wilderness permit is required year-round for backcountry and wilderness camping. You must have a permit to camp in any area, including trailside camps and cross-country and alpine zone camps. Group-size limits apply. The permit fee is $10.00 plus an additional $5.00 per person, and is good for up to 14 days.

• Camping along trails is permitted only at established trailside camps. No camping is permitted within ¼ mi of established trails or lakes with trailside camps.

• Cross-country camping is permitted ¼ mi or more away from trails and lakes with trailside campsites, and at least 100 feet away from lakes, streams and wetlands. Group-size limits apply to all zones (call ahead to check). During winter conditions (from October 1 through May 31), and when snow cover is greater than 2 feet, you may camp anywhere you wish, so long as you are more than 300 feet from buildings, 200 feet from roads and 100 feet from lakes and streams (except at Paradise, which requires five feet minimum snowcover and has other limits on party size and campsite location). You should discuss your cross-country, alpine and winter camping plans with a park ranger before your trip. He or she can suggest appropriate campsites.

• Alpine camping is permitted only on permanent snow or ice, or at designated sites. Do not clear tent sites on rocky, snow-free areas, as you may destroy very fragile alpine plants that cling to life in this zone. Do not camp on bare ground and vegetation within the boundaries of Muir snowfield between Pebble Creek and Anvil Rock. Check with park rangers to make sure your intended campsite is OK. Remember, without a permit, you aren't allowed to camp anywhere in the wilderness.

• Anyone intending to go above high camps (Muir, Schurman, Hazard), onto glaciers, or above 10,000 feet

Hikers pass through Indian Bar; Ohanapecosh Glacier and Whitman Crest are above. (Photo: Rob Lovitt)

elevation, must obtain a climbing permit and pay a $15.00 fee (or purchase a $25.00 annual pass). This includes Little Tahoma Peak.

Backcountry Safety

• Most trails above 4,000 feet are snow-covered until early July; routefinding can be difficult to impossible before melt out. A slip on steep snow can easily be fatal; learn self-arrest and bring an ice ax on early season hikes.

• Many major glacial rivers and streams will have washed-out bridges; the volumes of all glacial rivers and streams rise and fall each day. Be careful when fording creeks and rivers; the current can be deceptively swift and the water is dangerously cold.

• Expect fallen trees across many trails, and watch out for exposed rocks and tree roots which may be slippery when wet or icy.

• Be prepared for wet, cold, windy weather at all times; snow can fall at any time of year. Dress appropriately for the weather, whatever it may be.

• Boil or otherwise treat all water before driking.

Hikers should observe some precautions while visiting the backcountry of Mount Rainier National Park. Stay on the trail; don't try risky shortcuts. Be respectful of wildlife and "bear-proof" your campsite. Use smell-proof packaging for food, and don't advertise your food stores unless you want hungry visitors pillaging your campsite. Keep your distance from bears, deer and goats – remember, these are wild animals – and don't feed the animals.

On any hike, you should keep in mind that mountain weather can change very rapidly. No matter how clear a day begins, it may soon be raining or even snowing at any time of year. Go prepared! Bring adequate clothing, including rain and wind-resistant shells. Bring extra food and clothing, in case you are out longer than you anticipated. Bring the "Ten Essentials:" a map of the area, a compass, a flashlight with extra cells and bulbs, extra food, extra clothing, sunglasses, first aid kit, pocket knife, matches in waterproof container and firestarter – and know how to use them. Also bring something in case you get a headache, not an uncommon complaint for lowlanders visiting the alpine regions of Mount Rainier National Park.

Hypothermia

Hypothermia is a genuine risk for all backcountry hikers, even tourists on short hikes. This often-fatal lowering of the body temperature usually is brought on by continued exposure to low temperatures, high winds and rain, and often by a combination of all of these conditions, which are frequently encountered on and around Mount Rainier. To avoid hypothermia, bring proper clothing and wear it! Snack frequently to keep your metabolism rate high. If you are wet and cold, get dry and warm as soon as you can. Hypothermia is easier to prevent than to treat, so do your best to prevent it.

Hypothermia's symptoms include fatigue, awkwardness, chills, lethargy, irritability, clumsiness, uncontrolled shivering and slurred speech, though not necessarily in that order. Hypothermia victims often insist they are not experiencing any of these symptoms, even when it has become obvious to everyone else. Treating hypothermia requires quick action. If possible, stop, find shelter (erect a tent if you must), get the victim's wet clothes off and get him/her into a sleeping bag (with somebody undressed and warm if the victim appears seriously hypothermic, although decency permits the modest rescuer to wear underwear). Warm liquids should be given to conscious victims, but not to comatose victims. If the victim does not appear to recover, send someone for help immediately. The faster the victim's body temperature is raised, the better his or her chances of survival.

It is important to drink water often to avoid dehydration, which can set in easily on hot days and at high elevation. Although water is plentiful throughout the park, hikers and other backcountry users should bring their own. Mountain streams and lakes, however clear and cold, harbor many organisms that aren't friendly to humans. Purify any surface water you drink by boiling it for five or more minutes, or by using a water purification device guaranteed to prevent giardiasis and hepatitis. Also, help keep the park's water clean. Don't use any detergents for cleaning yourself or your dishes. Wash dishes more than 200 feet away from lakes and streams. Waste water should be disposed of where it will soak into the ground; however, don't dig holes, which may cause more damage than is prevented. It is best to remove food scraps and pour your waste water on vegetation.

Disposing of garbage and other waste products is a major concern in Mount Rainier National Park. The standard rule is, if you bring it in with you, you must take it out when you leave. Don't bury garbage or food leftovers, because critters will dig it up and leave it strewn all over the place. You may wish to burn paper products on your stove (but not plastic or styrofoam or other petroleum-based packaging!). Carry everything else out when you leave. Carry a plastic bag just for garbage. Don't toss your garbage into a crevasse or hide it under a rock. A good way to reduce garbage is to plan ahead and bring foods that don't require special packaging or those that have light, compactible or combustible packaging. Think ahead of ways to reduce waste and you won't have to worry so much about getting rid of it later on. When burning waste paper, be very careful! During periods of high fire hazard, don't risk starting a forest fire; pack it all out.

Human Waste Disposal

Human waste disposal is a major environmental problem in Mount Rainier National Park. A sign at the Paradise Ranger Station reminds visitors that more than six tons of human waste is deposited on the upper slopes of Mount Rainier each year. For those particularly inclined, the Park Service provides free plastic bags intended solely for human waste. Ideally, everyone would pack it out. However, in reality, few take the time or effort to do so (except climbers, who would rather carry it out than have their ropes dragged through it). Use pit toilets where they are provided. Alternatively, backcountry users should follow environmentally-sound waste disposal practices. Wherever possible, use toilet facilities. In lowland forests, it is recommended that you bury your waste in a 6-inch-deep hole dug in the surface soil. In higher-elevation areas, digging holes can cause severe damage to plant life. Here, and above timberline, it is recommended that you use the Park Service's blue bags whenever possible. Surface disposal is acceptable in low-use alpine and sub-alpine areas, but by all means, deposit your goods well away from water sources, campsites and trails. You should try to "go where no man has gone before." When using surface disposal methods, the Park Service suggests scattering and smearing feces with a stick to maximize exposure to air and sun and thus speed up decomposition. It sounds gross, but it is environmentally sound.

Trail Types

There are several crowded hikes that can be done in an hour or two, but if you really want to get away, try a longer hike in a remote corner of the park. Most hikers want views of the mountain. If views are what you are after, there are plenty of trails for you to follow, more than you can cover in a summer of weekend trips to the mountain. If you want solitude, though, be prepared to surrender views of the mountain, or to outwalk the masses.

The Park Service has designated several types of trails found within Mount Rainier National Park:

• Type A: Paved trails, such as those at Paradise and other tourist areas.

• Type B: Developed trails, such as the Wonderland Trail. These trails are improved and maintained by the Park Service.

• Type C: Also known as "way trails," these were created by frequent use, such as the trail leading from Mowich Lake to Knapsack Pass. They are maintained only as necessary to avoid unwanted erosion. The Park Service encourages visitors to use way trails whenever possible to avoid further adverse impact.

• Social Trails: These are trails created by frequent visitor use, such as paths encircling lakes and those leading to waterfalls and viewpoints (such as Third Burroughs Mountain). Social trails create and contribute to adverse impact. These trails are not maintained, and the Park Service prefers that you not use them.

• Interpretive Trails: These are self-guided "nature" trails, ranging from ¼ to 1 mile in length, as well as many short trails leading to viewpoints and other points of interest. For the most part, they are easy, well-marked trails that are suitable for all park visitors. Detailed interpretive booklets are available at some of these trailheads, for a small self-service fee.

Most trails are passable or snow-free from mid-July to late September. From Obtober to May (sometimes June), storms and snowfall should be anticipated. Many trails within the park are accessible in May or June; on most, however, snow lingers long into the summer. When hiking early in the year, be prepared for snow cover, and use great caution when crossing snow-covered streams or other obstacles, and when crossing potential avalanche paths. Don't venture onto glaciers or frozen lakes, no matter how safe they appear. Glissading accidents have claimed lives, so be sure you are on a safe slope with an adequate

A sign marks the Wonderland Trail at Aurora Lake in Klapatche Park. (Photo: Jeff Smoot)

runout; don't slide down snowslopes if you can't see what's below. In winter and spring, sometimes as late as June, beware of snow avalanches. All in all, July, August and September are the best months for hiking in Mount Rainier National Park. The weather can be hot, but trails are clear and the wildflowers blossoming.

Bridges and trails frequently are washed out by winter and spring flooding. Be sure to check current trail conditions at a Hiker Information Center before committing to a long hike. If the trail or a bridge is washed out and you can't find a safe passage, turn back.

Backcountry visitors must be aware that the listing of a trail in this guide does not mean it will be safe from hazards. Aside from other warnings contained in this book, hiking involves inherent risks that must be assumed by anyone following Mount Rainier's trails. Trail conditions can change overnight, and this guide makes no specific guarantees of a trail's present condition. This guide will try to warn of obvious or recurring trail hazards, where they are known; however, be aware that trail conditions are subject to change without warning. Know your limitations, and be prepared to adjust your course to accomodate changing conditions.

Don't be afraid to hike the trails of Mount Rainier National Park. The risks are but a few, the rewards many. Just be sure you know your abilities and limitations before you go trotting off into the wilderness and find yourself limping the last five miles back to the trailhead in darkness or, worse, awaiting a rescue from a high ridge in a rainstorm. If you find yourself in a hazardous situation, or caught in a storm, go back! You can come back another day more easily than you can summon a rescue. Careful planning can help you avoid most mishaps.

1   Klapatche Park ∎
Mileage: 5 mi/8 km
Duration: 4 hrs round trip from trailhead
Elevation Gain: 1,700 ft/520 m

The trail begins at St. Andrews Creek, switchbacking up Klapatche Ridge, and continuing along the ridge to meet the Wonderland Trail at Aurora Lake at 2½ mi. Stay on the trail, as these meadows are very fragile and suffering from shortcutting. A trailside camp is located just west of Aurora Lake. Continue from Aurora Lake ¼ mi south along the Wonderland Trail to St. Andrews Lake, nestled in a rocky basin. A climber's trail to Tokaloo Rock and Tahoma Glacier begins here. Go back the way you came, or loop out via Westside Road or Emerald Ridge Trail.

2   St. Andrews Park ∎
Mileage: 10¼ mi/16.5 km
Duration: 6 hrs round trip from trailhead
Elevation Gain: 2,500 ft/760 m

From the South Puyallup River on Westside Road, hike upriver a little more than 1½ mi to the Wonderland Trail just beyond South Puyallup Camp. Cross the river and continue north 3 mi, up broad switchbacks and along the open ridge crest, eventually descending through parkland to St. Andrews Lake, nestled in a rocky basin. In just over ¾ mi, as you descend the Wonderland Trail north along the parkland ridge, Klapatche Park and Aurora Lake can be found. You can loop out via Klapatche Park Trail.

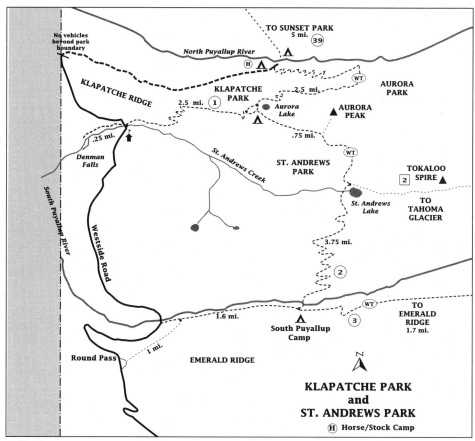

**KLAPATCHE PARK
and
ST. ANDREWS PARK**

Ⓗ Horse/Stock Camp

3 Emerald Ridge ■
Mileage: 6½ mi/25 km
Duration: 4 hrs round trip from trailhead
Elevation Gain: 2,000 ft/610 m

From Westside Road at the South Puyallup River, hike about 1½ mi along the river to South Puyallup Camp and the Wonderland Trail junction. Continue on the south side of the river up the rocky trail to the ridge crest directly above the terminus of the Tahoma Glacier. Beware, as the trail along the ridge crest is eroding. (The Park Service plans to reroute the trail to avoid this hazard.) Take care not to slip and fall several hundred feet to the glacier terminus. Eventually, the trail crests the ridge and drops into a rocky basin, where mountain goats are sometimes seen. The Wonderland Trail continues 2 mi down to a suspension bridge crossing Tahoma Creek. Because of storm and flood damage, the Tahoma Creek Trail remains closed. It is best to stop at the basin and hike back the way you came.

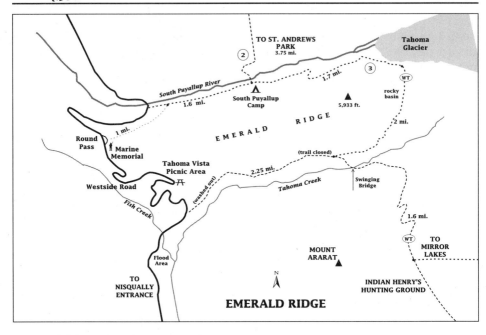

EMERALD RIDGE

4 Gobblers Knob ●

Mileage: 5 mi/8 km
Duration: 3 hrs round trip from trailhead
Elevation Gain: 1,565 ft/475 m

A short, popular climb to a lookout, with views of the Tahoma Glacier and Sunset Amphitheater of Mount Rainier. From Round Pass on Westside Road, hike a gradual 1 mi to Lake George and a popular campsite. Another mile of steep switchbacks reaches a ridge-top trail junction, where a final ½ mi north along the ridge crest reaches the lookout (5,485 ft/1672 m).

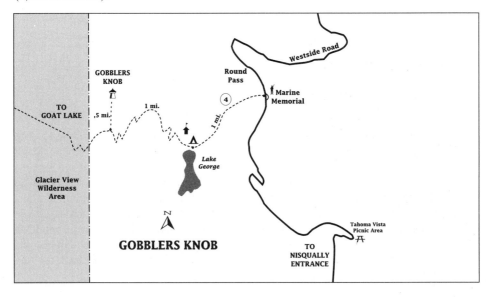

GOBBLERS KNOB

From the junction, a side trail drops 1½ mi west from the upper ridge of Gobblers Knob to Goat Lake in Glacier View Wilderness Area.

5 Kautz Creek ■
Mileage: 11½ mi/18.5 km
Duration: 6 hrs round trip
Elevation Gain: 3,200 ft/975 m

From the Kautz Creek exhibit and trailhead, hike about 1 mi through the washed-out creekbed to cross Kautz Creek. From the crossing, the trail climbs steadily, contouring the ridge crest above Tumtum Peak. Continue along the ridge to the slopes of Mount Ararat, then descend over a ridge a final ½ mi into Indian Henry's Hunting Ground to a junction with the Wonderland Trail. The total one-way distance is 5¾ mi. A possible one-way trip is to exit via the Wonderland Trail to Longmire.

6 Rampart Ridge ■
Mileage: 4¾ mi/7.6 km
Duration: 3 hr loop
Elevation Gain: 1,200 ft/365 m

Begin by walking clockwise (southwest) on Trail of the Shadows (½ mi loop) and climb about 2 mi up switchbacks to the crest of Rampart Ridge. Continue one mile along the ridge to the Wonderland Trail junction. It is possible to continue up Rampart Ridge 2¼ mi to Mildred Point, where you could loop down through Van Trump Park (the bridge sometimes is out) to Christine Falls trailhead, if you have a ride waiting. Most loop back the little more than 1½ mi to Longmire on the Wonderland Trail.

7 Indian Henry's Hunting Ground ■
Mileage: 12½ mi/20 km
Duration: 7 hrs round trip/overnight
Elevation Gain: 2,900 ft/885 m

From the junction of Paradise Highway and the Wonderland Trail (about ¼ mi above Longmire), hike west up the Wonderland Trail, climbing broad switchbacks for about 1½ mi to the junction with Rampart Ridge Trail. Continue down to Kautz Creek and over another ridge to Pyramid Creek, where you'll find a seldom-used campsite. The more popular Devil's Dream Camp is reached at 5¼ mi. Pass Squaw Lake and marshy meadows before climbing a "staircase" up a final rise to Indian Henry's Hunting Ground. The staircase-like trail was built to prevent erosion on this popular trail, and will give your knees something to remember on the hike out.

At 6¼ mi is a ranger cabin and the junction with Kautz Creek Trail. A customary side trip is to continue ¼ mi through the meadows to Mirror Lakes Trail junction, and follow that trail ¾ mi to Mirror Lakes.

This lovely parkland is very crowded on sunny summer weekends. Surprisingly, considering the volume of human traffic here, deer and other animals usually are present in abundance. Camping is restricted due to heavy use. Stay on the trail to avoid unnecessary erosion.

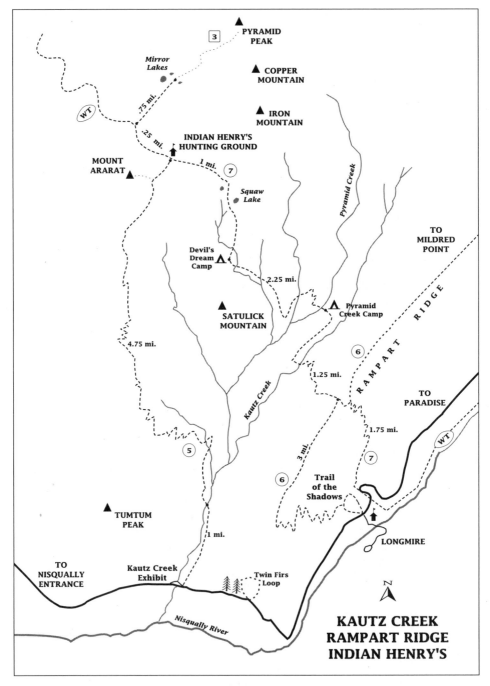

**KAUTZ CREEK
RAMPART RIDGE
INDIAN HENRY'S**

8 Eagle Peak ■
Mileage: 7 mi/11.25 km
Duration: 4 hrs round trip
Elevation Gain: 3,000 ft/915 m

Eagle Peak is the prominent mountain rising to the east above Longmire. The trail begins just across the Nisqually River suspension bridge, on the left (east). Ascend gradually, following numerous switchbacks up the initial steep slope, to the gap between Eagle Peak and Chutla Peak at 3½ mi, elevation 5,700 ft/1737 m. The short Class 2 scramble to the summit of Eagle Peak (via a gully and ramp on the southwest side) is not technically difficult, but should not be attempted by casual hikers without scrambling experience.

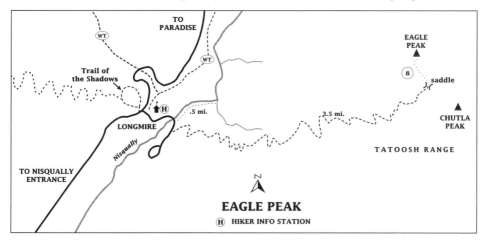

The view from Van Trump Park of the Tatoosh Range. (Photo: Pat Gentry)

9   Paradise River ●

Mileage: 4 mi/6.5 km
Duration: 2 hrs one way
Elevation Gain: 2,200 ft/670 m

The first portion of this historic trail, from Cougar Rock to Carter Falls, is an easy 2 mi round trip. The trail leads past Madcap Falls to Paradise Valley Camp at 2 mi. About ¾ mi higher is the Narada Falls Trail junction; stay left ¼ mi to Narada Falls viewpoint, a good stopping point if you have a ride waiting. The trail continues about 1 mi farther to Paradise, passing Stevens Canyon Road and joining The Lakes Trail ½ mi below Paradise.

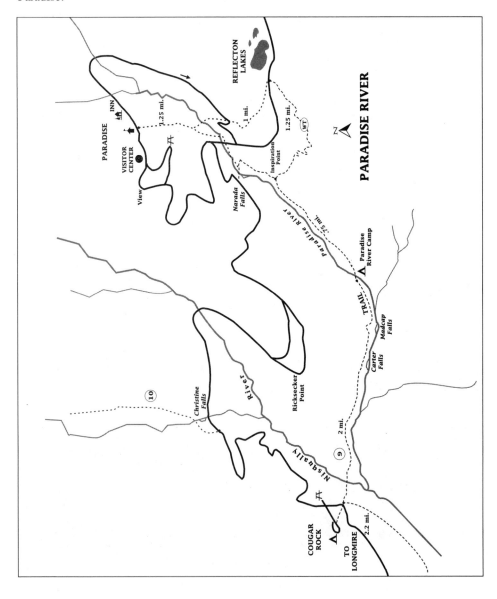

10 Comet Falls ●

Mileage: 4¾ mi/7.5 km
Duration: 3 hrs round trip
Elevation Gain: 2,000 ft/610 m

Comet Falls is the largest and most spectacular of Mount Rainier's accessible waterfalls. The trail begins just west of the Christine Falls bridge on Paradise highway, and crosses Van Trump Creek after ¼ mi. Climb 1¼ mi to the base of 320-foot-high Comet Falls. Van Trump Park is 1 mi above the falls.

It is possible to cross Van Trump Creek and go on to Mildred Point (½ mi from creek), or continue down 2¼ mi along Rampart Ridge to the Wonderland Trail junction. However, if the bridge is washed out, the creek crossing may be too much for any but experienced hikers.

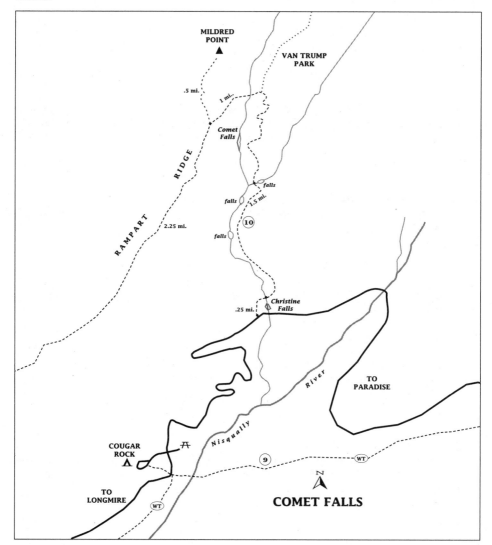

COMET FALLS

11 Paradise Meadows Hikes (Skyline Trail) ●

Mileage: 5 mi/8 km
Duration: 3 hr loop
Elevation Gain: 1,400 ft/425 m

Paradise has a confusing network of paved trails leading up from the visitor center and parking area. Most tourists are content to hike any old trail until they get tired, then turn around. Each variation of the trail has a name, which isn't as important as where each trail leads. Follow any trail you wish, as far as you wish to follow it. They all loop back to Paradise eventually.

Because this network of trails receives more foot traffic than any other within the park, it makes sense that it is partly paved – otherwise, the fragile meadows would have been trampled to death long ago. As it is, they still are recovering from substantial abuse. Although many visitors think, "It won't hurt for me to just step off here for a photo or to take this shortcut," if one out of every 100 visitors takes a shortcut, (considering thousands hike these trails on summer weekends), the meadows will again become criss-crossed with ugly swaths of erosion. Please stay on the trails! Off-trail hiking around Paradise is a citable offense. Also, don't pick flowers! It is illegal, not to mention selfish and destructive.

Alta Vista: Many tourist hikers reach Alta Vista, a prominent woody knoll visible just above the Paradise ranger station. There are numerous ways to reaching Alta Vista; the official version begins from the visitor center.

Deadhorse Creek Trail: Begin from the visitor center, and hike along Deadhorse Creek about 1 mi to Skyline Trail.

Moraine Trail: The Moraine Trail forks off from the Deadhorse Creek trail after ¾ mi, and descends to the Nisqually Glacier. Don't go too far, as the moraines are loose and prone to sliding. Stay off the glacier unless you are equipped for and experienced with glacier travel.

Narada Falls: Most visitors view Narada Falls only from above, but a better view is just down the trail from the parking area. The Narada Falls Trail continues up a little more than one mile along the Paradise River to Paradise, making a pleasant one-way excursion for those with a ride awaiting them at Paradise.

Nisqually Vista Trail: From the Paradise visitor center, this short loop trail leads westerly about one mile through meadows to a vista overlooking the Nisqually Glacier, with impressive views of Mount Rainier. The trail is comparatively flat and thus easier for the young and young at heart than most of the paved trails at Paradise.

Skyline Trail: The Skyline Trail is the longest route through and around Paradise Meadows, with its farthest point above Panorama Point. Begin from either the Paradise ranger station or visitor center, staying left of Alta Vista. Follow the signs pointing the way to Panorama Point. Pebble Creek Trail leads ½ mi above Panorama Point, and experienced hikers may continue upward across the Muir Snowfield to Camp Muir (elevation 10,188 ft/3105 m), along with summit-bound climbers. However, the route to Camp Muir (Off-trail Route 6) is not for casual hikers. The Skyline Trail continues eastward, past the Golden Gate, Sluiskin Falls and Stevens-Van Trump historical marker, looping its way back to Paradise. There are many possible variations to this hike, making it longer or shorter, but the trails are all well signed, and if you stay on them, you won't have to worry about getting lost – unless you can't find your car when you get back to Paradise.

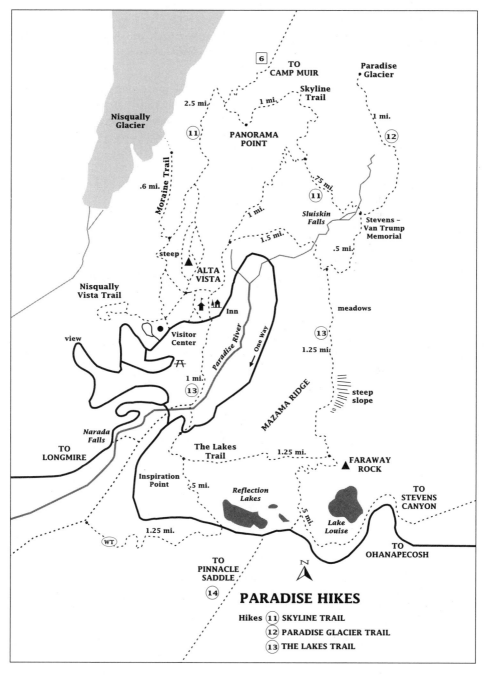

PARADISE HIKES

Hikes ⑪ SKYLINE TRAIL
⑫ PARADISE GLACIER TRAIL
⑬ THE LAKES TRAIL

12 Paradise Glacier ●
Mileage: 5¾ mi/9.25 km
Duration: 3 hr loop
Elevation Gain: 1,000 ft/300 m

From Paradise Inn, hike less than ½ mi along Skyline Trail to Myrtle Falls, and continue one mile to the junction with Mazama Ridge Trail. Continue up along Skyline Trail to Stevens-Van Trump historical monument, where the Paradise Glacier Trail leads about 1 mi to Paradise Glacier.

The famed Paradise Glacier ice caves are no more. Occasional timy meltwater openings appear in some years, but nothing like the deep blue grottoes of old to lure the tourists here. Although the glacier seems to be nothing more than a big snowfield, it is still hazardous. You should not venture onto the glacier, as hidden crevasses and ice caverns may still lurk beneath the harmless-looking snow.

13 The Lakes Trail – Mazama Ridge Loop ●
Mileage: 5¼ mi/8.5 km
Duration: 3 hrs one way
Elevation Gain: 1,100 ft/330 m

This hike combines The Lakes Trail and Mazama Ridge Trail in a pleasant loop beginning from either Paradise or Reflection Lakes.

From Paradise parking lot, hike south about ½ mi to Paradise River and the junction with Narada Falls Trail. Continue south, climbing out of Paradise Valley, crossing Paradise Valley Road, and hiking ½ mi to a junction with the High Lakes Trail. High Lakes leads 1¼ mi to the Mazama Ridge Trail above Faraway Rock. You can drop ½ mi to Reflection Lakes; a stiff ¾ mi climb past Faraway Rock returns you to the junction of the High Lakes Trail and Mazama Ridge Trail. Continue up Mazama Ridge Trail 1¼ mi to Skyline Trail, which leads back to Paradise by whichever variation you choose to follow, high or low, long or short.

14 Pinnacle Saddle ●
Mileage: 2¾ mi/4.5 km
Duration: 3 hrs round trip
Elevation Gain: 1,100 ft/330 m

This very popular hike begins from the parking turnout at Reflection Lakes along Stevens Canyon Road, about 2 mi from the Paradise Highway turnoff.

The trail ascends gradually along the west slope of Pinnacle Peak for just less than 1½ mi to a saddle between Pinnacle and Plummer Peaks, which offers expansive views of the south shoulder of Mount Rainier. From the saddle, some hikers scramble up a gully and rocky ridge to the summit of Pinnacle Peak, elevation 6,562 ft/2000 m. Although it is not a technical climb, it should not be attempted by anyone without experience on rocky mountain terrain. A fall here easily could be fatal. Rockfall from Pinnacle Peak has caused numerous injuries.

A way trail to Plummer Peak (elevation 6,370 ft/1,942 m) offers equal views with less risk. The "Mountaineers' Trail" on the northeast side of Pinnacle Peak should not be used, as the Park Service intends to restore this unnecessary social trail.

15 Snow Lake ●
Mileage: 2½ mi/4 km
Duration: 3 hrs round trip
Elevation Gain: 200 ft/60 m

This hike begins about ¾ mi east of Louise Lake turnout on Stevens Canyon Road. The trail begins steeply and levels off as it reaches The Bench, a broad plateau-like ridge. Bench Lake appears after ¾ mi. Continue down into the Unicorn Creek valley to Snow Lake, nestled in a rocky cirque of craggy Unicorn Peak, about 1¼ mi from the trailhead. This hike often is crowded on weekends. There is a trailside camp at Snow Lake.

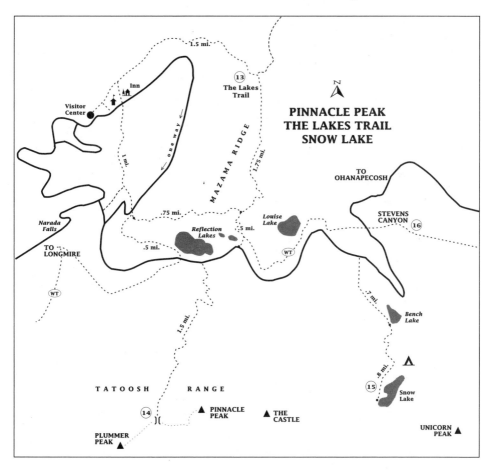

16 Stevens Canyon ■

Mileage: 6 mi/10 km
Duration: 4 hrs one way
Elevation Gain: 1,900 ft/575 m

The hike through Stevens Canyon follows a segment of the Wonderland Trail. Begin either at the picnic area just west of Box Canyon, or descend from Reflection Lakes. The description provided will be the ascent from Box Canyon.

From Box Canyon picnic area, a trail leads about ½ mi to the Wonderland Trail. The trail crosses Stevens Creek, continuing alongside the creek a gradual ¾ mi to Maple Creek Camp, below Maple Falls. After 2¼ mi, the trail passes Martha Falls, then climbs more noticeably for ½ mi to cross Stevens Canyon Road. Reflection Lakes lie 1¼ mi beyond.

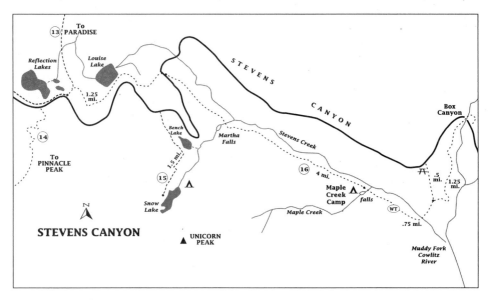

17 Indian Bar ■

Mileage: 15 mi/21 km
Duration: 10 hrs round trip/overnight
Elevation Gain: 2,000 ft/610 m

This long hike follows the Wonderland Trail along Cowlitz Divide, and often is done as a long day hike or overnight one-way hike in either direction. From Box Canyon on the Wonderland Trail, hike ¾ mi to Nickel Creek Camp. From Nickel Creek, the trail climbs steeply, switchbacking all the way to the crest of Cowlitz Divide at 2¼ mi. Continue, absorbing the stunning views, for 4¾ mi along the divide to Cowlitz Park. The trail leads through expansive subalpine meadows before dropping to Indian Bar shelter.

The trail continues for 3 mi to Panhandle Gap. One-way hikers will continue down through Summerland to White River road, an additional 6 mi (total one-way distance is about 17 mi).

18 Cowlitz Divide (Olallie Creek) ●
Mileage: 8½ mi/14 km
Duration: 5 hrs round trip
Elevation Gain: 2,400 ft/730 m

Begin at the trailhead about 1 mi inside the Stevens Canyon Entrance. The trail contours the east flank of Cowlitz Divide for about 2¾ mi to the not-often-used Olallie Creek Camp. After 1½ mi, the trail reaches Cowlitz Divide. Off-trail explorers can follow Olallie Creek southward from the campsite a gradual wooded mile to hidden Fir Lake. An unmaintained trail leads south along Cowlitz Divide to Backbone Ridge.

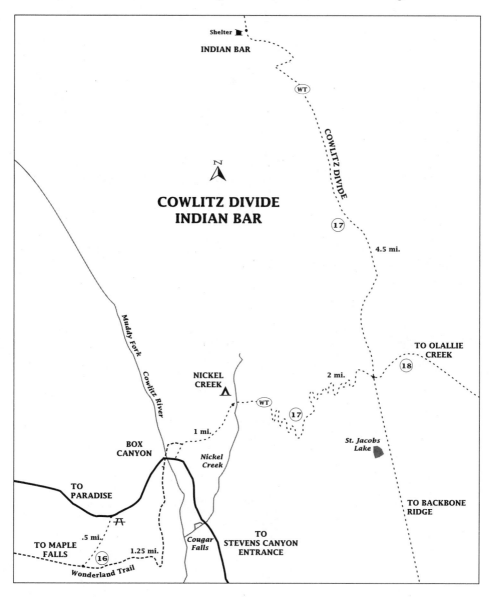

19   Eastside Trail ■

Mileage: 11¾ mi/19 km
Duration: 8 hrs one way/overnight
Elevation Gain: 3,200 ft/975 m

This long upriver trek begins from either Ohanapecosh Campground or the Grove of the Patriarchs trailhead, and climbs the Ohanapecosh River and its tributaries all the way to Chinook Pass.

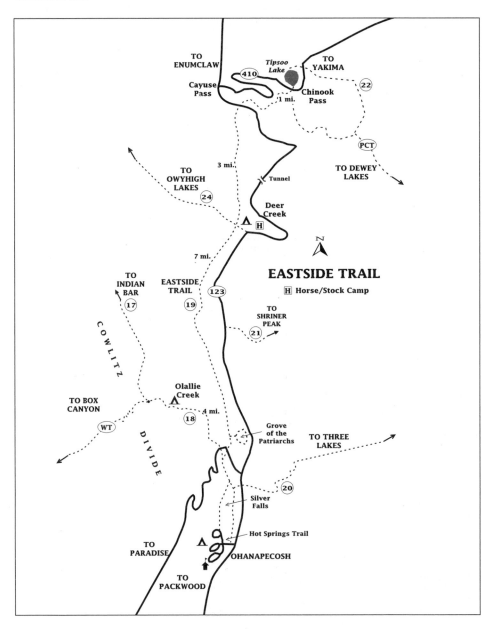

Begin at Ohanapecosh and hike about 2 mi along the river to Stevens Canyon Road, passing Silver Falls, a popular 3 mi loop from the campground. It is shorter to begin from Stevens Canyon Road, where the Grove of the Patriarchs Trail begins. Hike north along Ohanapecosh River ½ mi to a side trail (leading across the river to an island, home of "The Patriarchs," a stand of 1,000-year-old trees spared the ravages of fire by the surrounding river). After wandering 1½ mi through pristine old-growth forest, the trail crosses Olallie Creek. Cross the Ohanapecosh River 2¾ mi further, and continues alongside Chinook Creek for 3¼ mi to the confluence of Kotsuck, Deer and Chinook Creeks. Deer Creek Camp is a noisy but pleasant campsite – the camp is too easily reached via a short trail descending from Highway 123, and is scheduled to be relocated in 1992.

From Deer Creek Camp, cross the creeks and ascend through thinning forest 2¾ mi along Chinook Creek, crossing Highway 123 just below Cayuse Pass. After 1½ mi, the trail reaches Tipsoo Lake and Chinook Pass.

20 Laughingwater Creek – Three Lakes ■
Mileage: 11¾ mi/19 km
Duration: 8 hrs round trip
Elevation Gain: 2,600 ft/795 m

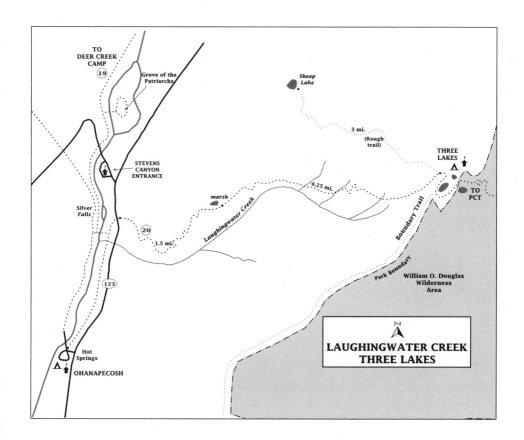

Laughingwater Creek Trail begins just south of the Stevens Canyon Entrance. Hike a crooked two miles to reach a swampy area alongside Laughingwater Creek. The trail continues around a shoulder of Sheep Mountain for 3¾ mi to Three Lakes. There is a ranger cabin and trailside camp here, just inside the park boundary.

The trail continues 1¾ mi to the Pacific Crest Trail, which can be hiked north for 11½ mi to Chinook Pass (Hike 40).

About ¼ mi west of Three Lakes, a way trail leads northwest along the ridge north of Laughingwater Creek to Sheep Lake, a very private destination reserved for those experienced in following poor trails.

The long-abandoned East Boundary Trail follows the ridge south of Laughingwater Creek, along the approximate line of the park boundary. It is a challenging and lonesome path for those inclined to follow it.

21 Shriner Peak ■

Mileage: 8¼ mi/13.25 km
Duration: 5 hrs round trip
Elevation Gain: 3,400 ft/1035 m

The Shriner Peak Trail begins north of the Stevens Canyon Entrance on Highway 123, a mile north of Panther Creek. It isn't a popular hike, being fairly remote and steep, but it offers splendid views of Mount Rainier.

In the first 1 mi, contour around the south ridge of Shriner Peak, and traverse 1½ mi above Panther Creek before switching-back ¾ mi to the ridge crest. Continue along the gradual ridge and across a high basin, and enjoy impressive views of the east side of Mount Rainier. A series of short, steep switchbacks leads a final ¼ mi to the summit lookout.

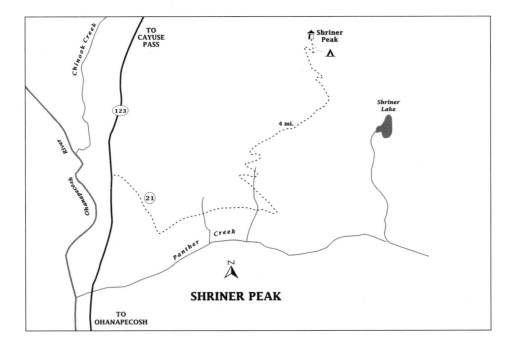

SHRINER PEAK

Elk herds sometimes are seen in this area of the park, especially later in the summer. Although this commonly is done as a day hike, a trailside camp is located about 200 yards south of the lookout for overnighters. Off-trail hikers can descend eastward to Shriner Lake.

22 Naches Peak Loop ●
Mileage: 4¼ mi/6.5 km
Duration: 3 hr loop
Elevation Gain: 650 ft/200 m

Tipsoo Lake and Chinook Pass offer fine views of the eastern flank of Mount Rainier and its intervening ridges (Governors Ridge, Cowlitz Chimneys and Little Tahoma Peak). A ½-mi trail encircles the lake.

The Naches Peak Loop starts from either Chinook Pass or Tipsoo Lake. From Tipsoo Lake, hike south, climbing for ¾ mi to a shoulder of Naches Peak. The trail curves east from here, and in ¾ mi joins the Pacific Crest Trail near the park boundary. Follow the Pacific Crest Trail outside the park, contouring north alongside Naches Peak for about 2 mi to Chinook Pass. Drop down to Tipsoo Lake in ¼ mi.

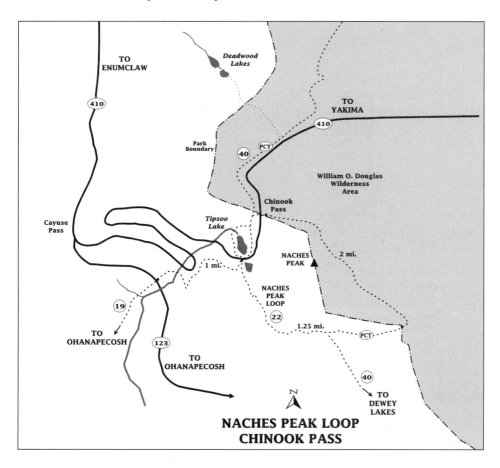

**NACHES PEAK LOOP
CHINOOK PASS**

23 Crystal Lakes ■
Mileage: 6½ mi/8 km
Duration: 5 hrs round trip
Elevation Gain: 2,300 ft/700 m

The trail begins ½ mi north of the White River Road fork on Highway 410, and climbs steeply from the start. Bring plenty of water so you don't overheat. After about 1½ mi, at the point where the trail splits, the going gets easier.

The left fork leads 1¼ mi to Lower Crystal Lake, and beyond to Upper Crystal Lake in another ½ mi. There are campsites at both lakes. About 1½ mi above the lakes is a junction with the Pacific Crest Trail, which can be followed south to Chinook Pass.

The righthand fork leads 2½ mi to the summit of Crystal Peak (6,595 ft/2010 m), overlooking Crystal Lakes and the White River valley, with views of Little Tahoma and the Emmons Glacier.

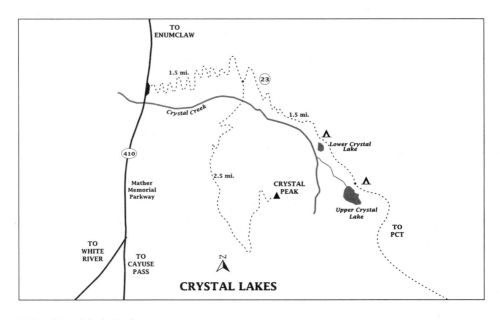

CRYSTAL LAKES

24 Owyhigh Lakes ■
Mileage: 5½ mi/8 km
Duration: 3 hrs round trip
Elevation Gain: 1,400 ft/426 m

The trail begins about 2½ mi inside the White River Entrance, climbing gradually and contouring east to the ridge of Tamanos Mountain. From the final switchback at 1½ mi, the trail traverses the flanks of Tamanos Mountain for ½ mi to Tamanos Creek Camp, and in another ¾ mi reaches the lakes.

Owyhigh Lakes also can be approached from Highway 123 at Deer Creek. This less-traveled path climbs 4 mi along Kotsuck Creek before dropping ¾ mi to the lakes, and makes for a good one-way hike if you have a ride waiting.

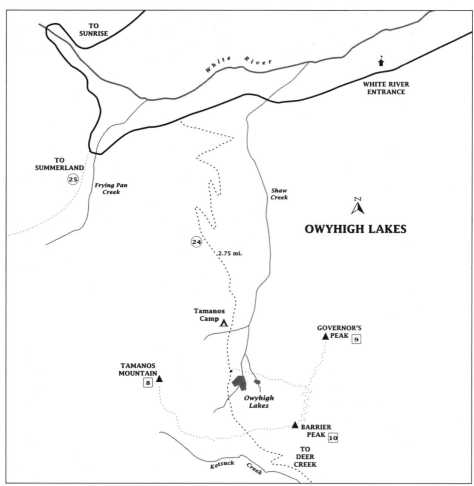

25 Summerland ■

Mileage: 8¾ mi/14 km
Duration: 5 hrs round trip
Elevation Gain: 1,100 ft/335 m

The trail begins just beyond the point where White River Road crosses Fryingpan Creek. It parallels Fryingpan Creek for more than 4 mi; the series of switchbacks runs about halfway to the creek crossing. Once across the creek, it's a short walk to Summerland shelter.

Panhandle Gap is 1¼ mi higher, offering perhaps the most reliable mountain goat viewing within the park. One-way hikers can continue 3 mi farther to Indian Bar and along the Cowlitz Divide to Stevens Canyon Road (17 mi total).

Summerland ranks with Spray Park in popularity, and although the meadows are recovering from past abuses, they still are quite fragile. Take care.

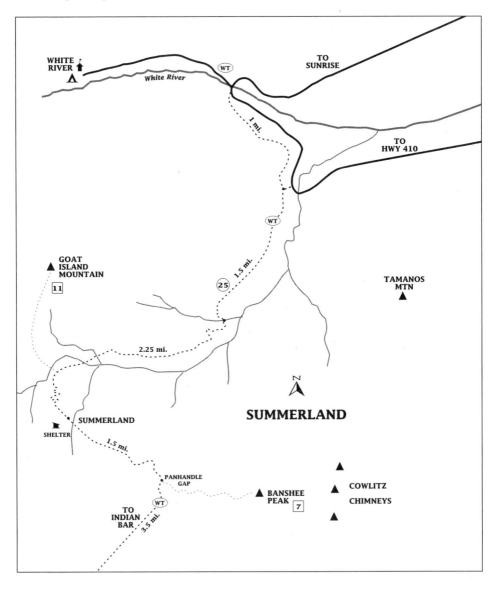

26 Glacier Basin ●

Mileage: 6 mi/10 km
Duration: 3 hrs round trip
Elevation Gain: 1,700 ft/520 m

This hike begins from White River Campground. The path is wide and easy to follow, with only a few steep sections.

The trail leads 1½ mi to a junction with the Emmons Moraine Trail – a short hike to views of Emmons Glacier and Little Tahoma Peak. Continue 1 mi along the river to the junction with Burroughs Mountain Trail. The Glacier Basin Trail stays left and reaches Glacier Basin Camp in ½ mi. A climbers' trail leads west to St. Elmo Pass, where you'll find views of Winthrop Glacier and Curtis Ridge.

A longer loop trip (about 13 mi) may be taken over Burroughs Mountain, returning (and descending) to White River Campground via the Wonderland Trail.

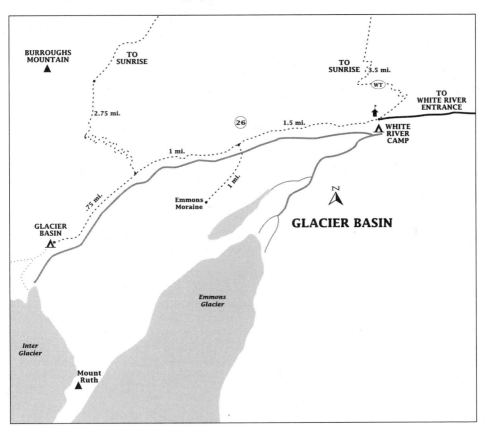

27 Palisades Lakes – White River Park ■
Mileage: 7½ mi/12 km
Duration: 5 hrs round trip/overnight
Elevation Gain: 1,600 ft/490 m

The trail through White River Park begins from Sunrise Point. Descend east along Sunrise Ridge about ¼ mi, then descend ¼ mi to a side trail leading to Sunrise Lake. The trail continues for 1½ mi to Clover Lake, then crosses a divide to Dick Lake (2 mi). Here, you'll find a trailside camp at Harry Lake and a short side trail to Hidden Lake. At 3¾ mi point, Upper Palisades Lake, with a trailside camp and views of the craggy Palisades is reached.

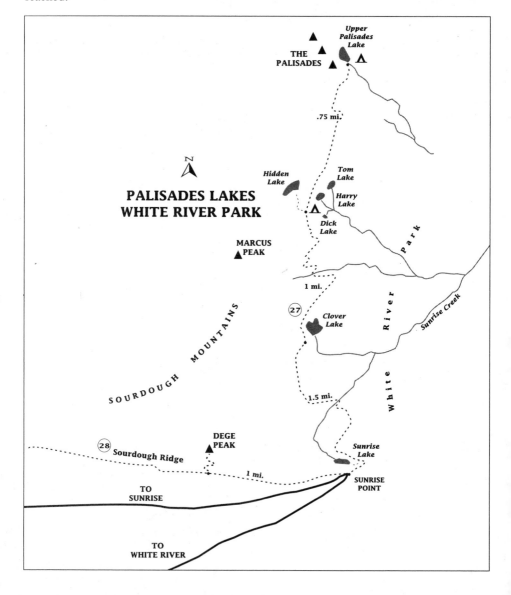

28 Sunrise Area Trails ●

Mileage: 1¼ to 3 mi/2 km to 5 km
Duration: 1 to 2 hrs

Sunrise and Yakima Park offer several short hiking opportunities. Don't leave the trail here, as the meadows are very fragile and can all too easily be damaged. The trails are plenty wide, and very easy to follow. There are many possible loop hike variations. Stay on the trails; off-trail hiking in the Sunrise area is a citable offense. This includes Burroughs Mountain!

Sourdough Ridge: Sourdough Ridge marks the northern boundary of Yakima Park. This ridge of mountains can be traversed from Sunrise Point to Fremont Peak on trails. A self-guided loop that begins at Sunrise parking area leads to the ridge crest and back. Many visitors continue eastward along the ridge crest to Dege Peak, about 1¼ mi miles distant. The summit of Dege Peak is accessible from Sunrise Point in just over one mile, making it one of the most-often climbed mountains within Mount Rainier National Park. An alternative is to continue west along the ridge to Frozen Lake, located one mile from Sunrise.

Emmons Vista Trail: From the visitor center, head south a short distance to the point where the trail forks. The east trail passes Emmons Vista in ¼ mi, offering wonderful views of Mount Rainier, Emmons Glacier and White River Valley. Continue for one mile to Silver Forest, a stand of silvered firs, and more views of Mount Rainier.

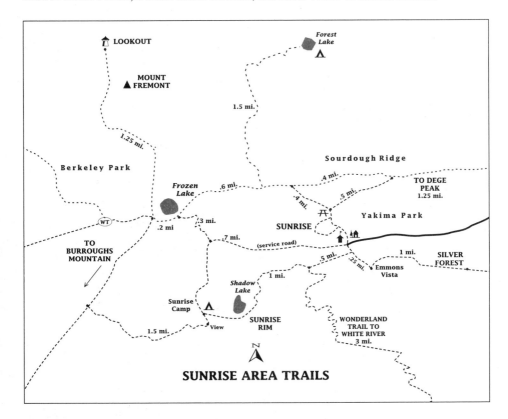

SUNRISE AREA TRAILS

Sunrise Rim: From Sunrise, hike south to where signs direct you to the Wonderland Trail and Sunrise Camp. The trail contours around the rim for ½ mi to the Wonderland Trail, which drops about 3 mi to White River Campground. Stay high, and in a mile you'll reach Shadow Lake and Sunrise Camp. From here, trails continue to Burroughs Mountain and Frozen Lake. You can loop back via Sourdough Ridge to Sunrise. There are many possible loop variations; take your pick.

Burroughs Mountain: Burroughs Mountain offers good views of the Winthrop Glacier and Curtis Ridge. The trail begins at Sunrise. Hike the Sunrise Rim Trail 1½ mi to Shadow Lake, and continue 1½ mi to First Burroughs Mountain and a junction with the trail from Frozen Lake. Or, hike 1¼ mi along the Sunrise access road to Frozen Lake, then go ¾ mi to the junction mentioned above, saving about 1 mi distance. This trail has a steep snow crossing until August most years. From First Burroughs Mountain, the trail continues about ¾ mi to Second Burroughs Mountain and the Meaney Memorial. Other loops of varying distances are possible from Sunrise and White River Campground.

The true summit of Burroughs Mountain is a short off-trail walk to the west. This social trail suffers from too much human trampling, so travel to Third Burroughs Mountain is discouraged by the Park Service and you may be cited for hiking there.

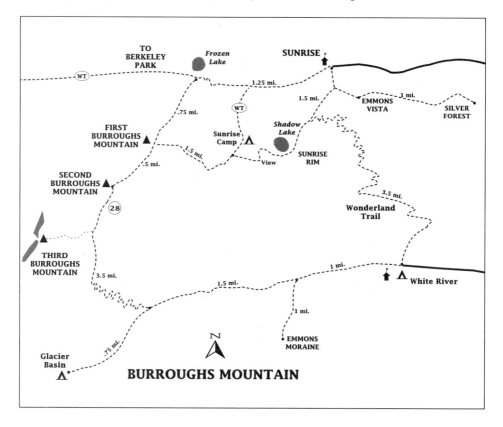

BURROUGHS MOUNTAIN

29 Huckleberry Creek ▲

Mileage: 10½ mi/17 km
Duration: 7 hrs one way/overnight
Elevation Gain: 3,700 ft/1125 m

Approach via Highway 410 from Enumclaw or Sunrise. About 10 mi north of the park boundary, turn up Forest Service Road 73, which leads southwest through logged forest. Drive 5½ mi, then turn left onto Road 7340, which is followed to the trailhead. Hike through regrown forest to the park boundary, and a historic ranger cabin (unmanned). The trail continues through old-growth forest for several miles alongside Huckleberry Creek, crossing Ada Creek and Josephine Creek. At 8 mi from the trailhead, after a stiff

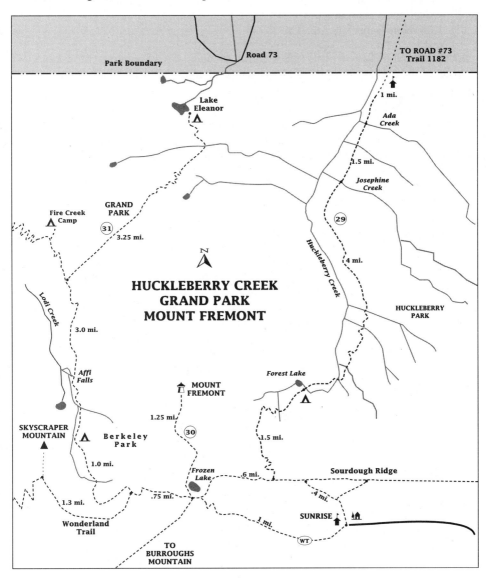

climb from the creek, you'll find Forest Lake and its usually uncrowded trailside camp. Continue from the lake through western Huckleberry Basin, climbing another 1½ mi to Sourdough Ridge and long-awaited views of Mount Rainier. Descend the crowded trail ¾ mi to Sunrise. You also can begin from Sunrise and hike downstream; easier, but less dramatic.

Be sure to have a ride waiting at either end, because it's a long way back. Some shuttle cars between the trailhead and Sunrise, but it's a hassle. Some hike only from Sunrise to Forest Lake and back; this the most scenic section of the trail and is only 4½ mi round trip.

30   Mount Fremont Lookout ●
Mileage: 4 ¾ mi/7.5 km
Duration: 3 hrs round trip
Elevation Gain: 800 ft/250 m

Mount Fremont lookout occupies the westernmost point of the Sourdough Mountains, with expansive and impressive views of Mount Rainier, Berkeley Park and Grand Park.

There are several ways to reach the lookout from Sunrise. The shortest is to hike along Sourdough Ridge west to Frozen Lake (about 1¼ mi). From the trail junction, ascend north to the crest of Sourdough Ridge, near Mount Fremont's true summit. You'll be treated to views all along the way to the lookout, which is reached after 1¼ mi (elevation 7,181 ft/2189 m). Stay on the trail here; this is a very fragile area.

31   Grand Park ■
Mileage: 13¾ mi/22 km
Duration: 8 hrs round trip/overnight
Elevation Gain: 1,850 ft/565 m

Grand Park is a wide meadow sitting atop a flat-topped lava flow, and is regarded by many as the park's finest meadow. Hike about 1 mi from Sunrise to Frozen Lake, and continue ¾ mi through tundra-like meadows to the Northern Loop Trail junction at Berkeley Park. Descend to Berkeley Park Camp in 1 mi. Affi Falls is passed ½ mi farther. The trail climbs gradually into the wide, open meadows of Grand Park, reaching the Lake Eleanor trail junction in 3 mi. Wander through the vast meadow (staying on the trail, if you please) to reach remote Lake Eleanor in 3¼ mi.

Camping is restricted in the fragile meadow. Stay at Lake Eleanor, Fire Creek or Berkeley Park trailside camps.

Note: Road damage frequently affect access to Carbon River and Ipsut Creek area hikes. Ipsut Creek campground may be accessible to foot traffic only, until road repairs are completed. Call (360) 569-2211 to check current road status before your trip.

32 Green Lake ●

Mileage: 4 mi/6 km
Duration: 2 hrs round trip
Elevation Gain: 1,000 ft/305 m

A short, steep, sometimes crowded hike to a quiet lake. No views of the mountain here, just a peaceful walk through a tranquil old-growth forest with a lovely lake at trail's end.

The well-marked trailhead is about 3½ mi from the Carbon River entrance. Ascend gradually 1 mi through lowland forest to Ranger Falls, and more steeply for 1 mi to the lake.

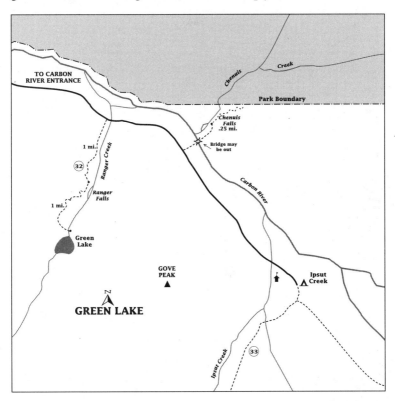

33 Ipsut Creek ■

Mileage: 8 mi/13 km
Duration: 5 hrs round trip

A memorable hike through pristine forest. There are no impressive views until Ipsut Pass, but this is one of the finest forest hikes in the park.

From Carbon River Road's end, hike ¼ mi to the junction with the Carbon River Trail. The trail climbs gradually along Ipsut Creek for 3½ mi, then crosses over the creek and climbs the opposite valley slope, switchbacking through marmot-infested talus below steep cliffs for ½ mi to Ipsut Pass. A mammoth Alaska-cedar stands just beyond the creek crossing.

From the pass, you can continue 1¾ mi to Tolmie Peak. One-way hikers can go on to Mowich Lake to meet their transportation. Continue in an 18 mi loop through Spray and Seattle Parks.

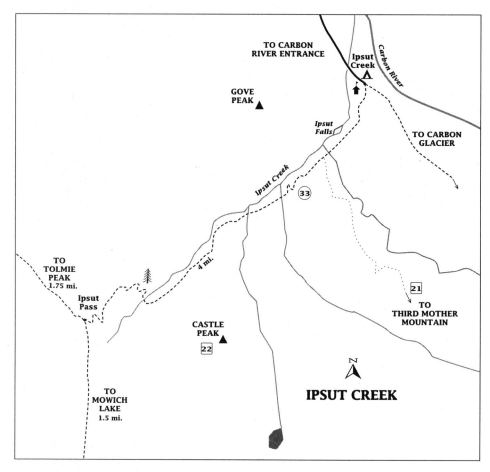

TO CARBON RIVER ENTRANCE

Ipsut Creek

Carbon River

GOVE PEAK ▲

Ipsut Falls

TO CARBON GLACIER

Ipsut Creek

(33)

TO TOLMIE PEAK 1.75 mi.

4 mi.

21

Ipsut Pass

TO THIRD MOTHER MOUNTAIN

CASTLE PEAK ▲

22

N

TO MOWICH LAKE 1.5 mi.

IPSUT CREEK

34 Seattle Park ■
Mileage: 9¼ mi/15 km
Duration: 6 hrs round trip/overnight
Elevation Gain: 2,600 ft/800 m

Seattle Park, along with Spray and Mist Parks, occupies the southeast section of a vast parkland between the Carbon and Mowich Rivers.

From Ipsut Creek Campground, hike the Carbon River Trail 3 mi to Carbon River Camp at Cataract Creek. Turn west along the Wonderland Trail and hike along the creek another 1 mi to Cataract Falls. The trail veers off alongside Marmot Creek, with switchbacks aplenty, another ¾ mi to Cataract Valley Camp.

Off-trail exploration through the parkland is very enjoyable, but keep in mind that overuse is damaging to the fragile meadows. Don't leave the trail if you don't need to do so. Stay off the Russell and Flett Glaciers unless you are equipped for glacier travel.

Continue in an 18 mi loop through Spray Park to Mowich Lake and down Ipsut Creek if you have a full day or two.

35 Mystic Lake ■
Mileage: 15 mi/24 km
Duration: 10 hrs round trip/overnight
Elevation Gain: 4,100 ft/1250 m

Begin from Ipsut Creek, hiking the Carbon River Trail 3 mi to the swinging bridge. Trail washouts have occurred along the river's edge in the past, and may occasionally make the final 1/2 mi before the bridge difficult or hazardous. Cross the bridge carefully and continue up the Wonderland Trail to behold the snout of the Carbon Glacier. The trail passes beneath steep cliffs here; there is risk of rockfall, so hurry along.

Dick Creek Camp lies 1¼ mi beyond the bridge. The trail continues climbing along the Carbon Glacier and Moraine Creek into Moraine Park, reaching Mystic Pass 3 mi from Dick Creek. A quick ½-mi descent reaches Mystic Lake. A ranger cabin and Mystic Camp are just east from the lake.

36 Northern Loop Trail ▲
Mileage: 33 mi/52 km
Duration: 8 hrs round trip to Windy Gap; 3 days entire loop
Elevation Gain: 3,400 ft/1035 m to Windy Gap; 7000 ft/2134 m entire loop

There are many off-trail explorations along this trail. If you stay awhile, complete the Northern Loop Trail for a 33 mile loop through Mount Rainier's northern parkland.

From Ipsut Creek, hike 2 mi to a side trail, which heads east and crosses Carbon River in ¼ mi. Unfortunately, the crossing sometimes is washed out, so you may have to continue 1¼ mi farther to the swinging bridge, and return 1¼ mi on the other side of the river. From here, the trail ascends steeply through deep forest via many switchbacks for 3¾ mi to Yellowstone Cliffs Camp. Ascend a gradual ¾ mi through open meadows to Windy Gap.

From Windy Gap, you can descend east a short way to Independence Ridge Trail, which leads north (1 mi) to Natural Bridge, a unique free-standing arch. This trail is unmaintained from Natural Bridge, but can be followed a bit farther to Oliver Lake. A round trip to Natural Bridge is 16 mi/25.5 km – a long day or overnight trip.

Continue along the Northern Loop Trail to Lake James ranger cabin, which is about ¼ mi south of Lake James. The Lake James campsite has been permanently closed. A new campsite, Redstone camp, is located near the ranter cabin.

Ambitious hikers can complete the Northern Loop Trail by dropping steeply down from Lake James to Mowich Fork White River, ascending to Grand Park, then climbing through Berkeley Park to meet the Wonderland Trail, which leads to Mystic Lake and down to Ipsut Creek Campground. The entire Northern Loop Trail is about 35 mi/56 km if you have to cross the swinging bridge both ways (33mi/52 km if you don't), and is best done in three days or more. When the bridge is out, you can shave off a couple of miles by beginning the loop at Sunrise, via Frozen Lake.

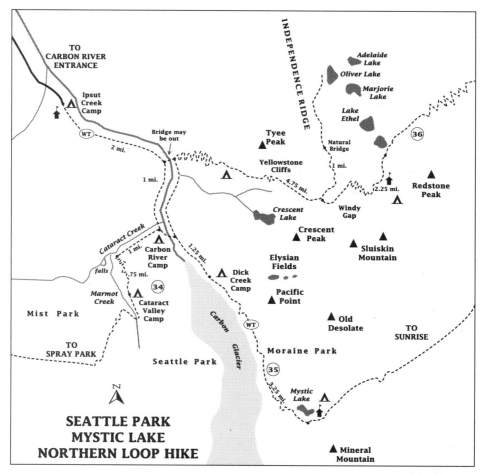

TO CARBON RIVER ENTRANCE

Ipsut Creek Camp

WT

2 mi.

Bridge may be out

1 mi.

INDEPENDENCE RIDGE

Adelaide Lake

Oliver Lake

Marjorie Lake

Lake Ethel

Tyee Peak

Natural Bridge

36

1 mi.

Yellowstone Cliffs

4.75 mi.

12.25 mi.

Redstone Peak

Crescent Lake

Windy Gap

Cataract Creek

1 mi.

Carbon River Camp

1.25 mi.

Crescent Peak

Sluiskin Mountain

falls

.75 mi.

34

Dick Creek Camp

Elysian Fields

Marmot Creek

Cataract Valley Camp

Pacific Point

Mist Park

Carbon Glacier

WT

Old Desolate

TO SUNRISE

TO SPRAY PARK

Seattle Park

Moraine Park

35

N

3.25 mi.

Mystic Lake

SEATTLE PARK
MYSTIC LAKE
NORTHERN LOOP HIKE

Mineral Mountain

Sluiskin Mountain's east summit, The Chief, as seen from near Windy Gap. (Photo: Pat Gentry)

37 Tolmie Peak ●

Mileage: 6¼ mi/8 km
Duration: 4 hrs round trip
Elevation Gain: 1,000 ft/305 m

Tolmie Peak sits above pretty Eunice Lake just north of Mowich Lake and offers spectacular views of the northwest shoulder of Mount Rainier. Begin from about ½ mi up the Mowich Lake road, at the well-marked trailhead.

The trail climbs from the lake to reach Ipsut Pass at about 2 mi. Contour along the ridge ¾ mi to Eunice Lake. The trail takes off steeply for another ¾ mi to the lookout atop Tolmie Peak (elevation 5,939 ft/1810 m); the true summit is ¼ mi east, a Class 2 scramble from the lookout. The lookout also is reached easily via Ipsut Creek Trail in 5¾ mi/9 km. No camping is allowed in the heavily impacted Eunice Lake Basin. Please stay on the trail here.

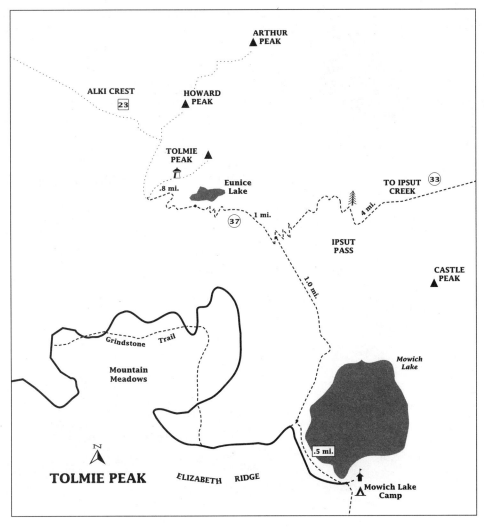

38 Spray Park ■

Mileage: 6¼ mi/10 km
Duration: 4 hrs round trip
Elevation Gain: 1,000 ft/305 m

A very popular hike to one of the most scenic areas of the park. In early summer, Spray Park often is blanketed in wildflowers, luring photographers, flower lovers and wanderers alike. Unfortunately, as is true of any special area, Spray Park is being "loved to death." Spray Park is the most accessible subalpine meadow in Mount Rainier National Park, and regularly is swarmed by the masses on sunny summer weekends. If everyone stayed on the trail, there wouldn't be a problem. But shortcutting, hiking around snowcovered trail sections, random explorations, improper waste disposal and other unwise user practices are seriously impacting these meadows. The Park Service has scheduled restoration work for 1992 or 1993. Please stay on the trail!

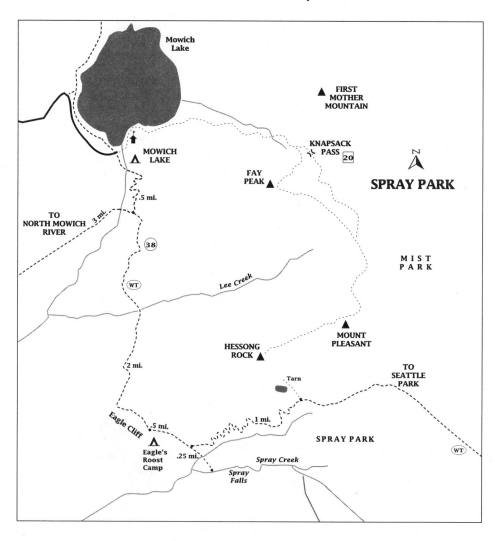

39 Golden Lakes – Sunset Park ■

Mileage: 15½ mi/19 km
Duration: 9 hrs round trip/overnight
Elevation Gain: 1,300 ft/400 m

There are two customary approaches to Sunset Park and Golden Lakes. The route from Westside Road is the shortest, but when the road is closed to auto traffic, the Mowich Lake/Paul Peak approach is best.

From Westside Road near Klapatche Point (the road's end for vehicular traffic), hike 2¾ mi along the remnants of the road to North Puyallup Camp. Cross the narrow river gorge and continue for 3 mi, gradually climbing and contouring through forest before the trail swings into open meadows at the Silver Fir Forest. Golden Lakes ranger cabin and trailside camp is 2 mi farther.

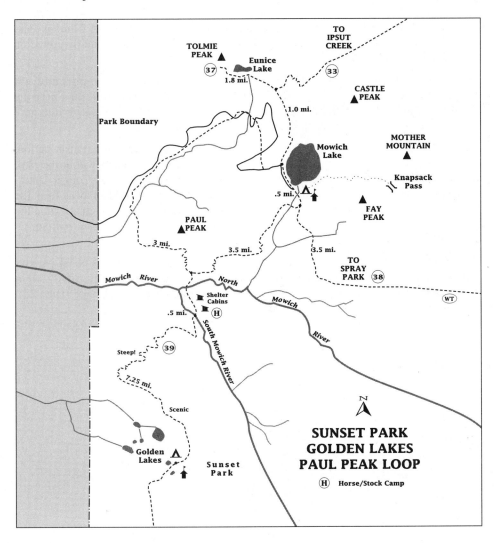

Sunset Park also may be reached from Mowich Lake via the Wonderland Trail. Drop ¼ mi south from Mowich Lake to the Spray Park Trail junction. Continue on the Wonderland Trail, contouring and switchbacking downward through forest, to Paul Peak Trail junction (3½ mi from Mowich Lake). Descend to North Mowich River and in ½ mi cross South Mowich River (shelter cabins near both river crossings), where the trail reenters forest and climbs lower Colonade Ridge via 3½ mi of relentless switchbacks to a broad saddle. Here, the trail enters Sunset Park, contouring a gradual 3 mi to Golden Lakes.

40 Pacific Crest Trail ▲

Mileage: 17¼ mi/27 km one way from Stevens Canyon to Chinook Pass
Duration: Long day or overnight
Elevation Gain: 4,500 ft/1371 m
Elevation Loss: 1,000 ft/305 m

The Pacific Crest Trail follows the national park's east boundary south of Chinook Pass for over 11 miles. Stock and pets are permitted on the PCT, but pets are not permitted on Laughingwater Creek Trail.

Begin either from Highway 123 just north of Ohanapecosh Campground via Laughingwater Creek Trail (Hike 20), or from Chinook Pass. The PCT runs near the divide separating Mount Rainier National Park and William O. Douglas Wilderness Area, climbing and dropping back and forth over the crest all along the way.

This trip can be done in a long day by ambitious hikers with arranged transportation. Most prefer a more leisurely pace, taking two or three days. Camping within the park along the PCT is not permitted; camping near Two Lakes, American and Cougar Lakes, and Dewey Lakes is permitted, but your campsite must be at least 100 feet away from the lakeshore and 100 feet from the trail. Do not camp at Anderson Lake, which is within the park boundary. No permit presently is required for overnight camping in William O. Douglas Wilderness.

The PCT continues north from Chinook Pass, but this section of the trail is not as popular as that south of the pass. The trail leads 3½ mi to Sheep Lake, then climbs a stiff 1½ mi to Sourdough Gap, from where a side trail drops 1½ mi to Upper Crystal Lake (Hike 23), and reaches Highway 410 in a final 3¼ mi descent.

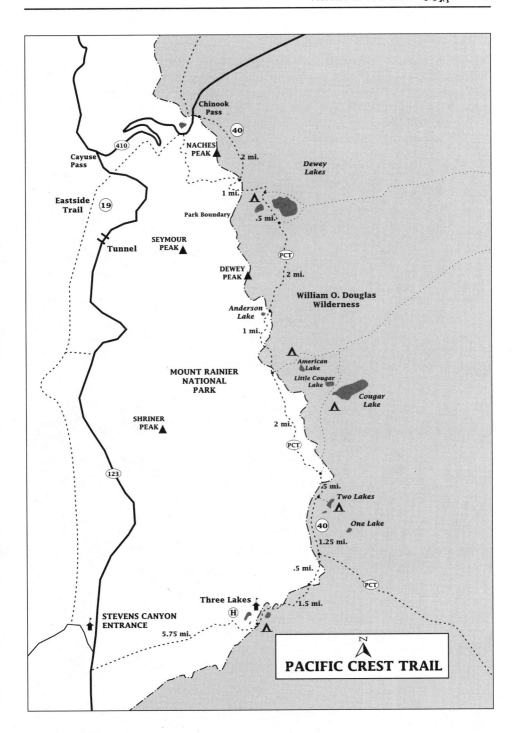

Chinook
Pass

40

NACHES
PEAK ▲   2 mi.

410

Cayuse
Pass

*Dewey
Lakes*

Eastside
Trail   19

1 mi.

Park Boundary

.5 mi.

SEYMOUR
PEAK ▲

Tunnel

PCT

DEWEY
PEAK ▲   2 mi.

**William O. Douglas
Wilderness**

*Anderson
Lake*

1 mi.

MOUNT RAINIER
NATIONAL
PARK

A
*American
Lake*

*Little Cougar
Lake*

*Cougar
Lake*

A

SHRINER
PEAK ▲

2 mi.

PCT

.5 mi.

Two Lakes

A

40   *One Lake*

1.25 mi.

123

.5 mi.

PCT

Three Lakes   1.5 mi.

H

STEVENS CANYON
ENTRANCE   5.75 mi.

A

N

PACIFIC CREST TRAIL

Horse and Stock Trails

About 100 miles of park trails are open for horse and stock use. However, the park is infrequently visited by stock parties because of several factors, including late snow cover, swollen glacial rivers, irregular, narrow trails – and because the trails open to stock are not among the park's most scenic. If you wish to bring stock into the park, contact the Park Service for current limitations at (360) 569-2211, or check the Mount Rainier National Park homepage for current limitations.

A lone hiker enjoys a meadow below Mt. Rainier. (Photo: Rob Lovitt)

Chapter Five:
The Wonderland Trail

The Wonderland Trail is to hikers what the summit climb of Mount Rainier is to climbers — the ultimate Mount Rainier experience. For this reason, a separate chapter of this book, albeit brief, will be devoted solely to the Wonderland Trail. This varied network of trails encircles the mountain, passing through high meadows, over stark ridges, through forested valleys, across raging rivers, alongside creaking glaciers and pristine lakes, through open country and dense forest, with frequent views of Mount Rainier, both up close and distant. The entire loop is about 93 miles long, and takes the average hiker 10 to 14 days to complete. Many do the trail in sections, taking several years to make the entire circumnavigation of the mountain. A few individuals have completed the hike in much shorter time (the latest unofficial "record," set by a seasonal park ranger in 1990, is 27 hours, 56 minutes!), but those not wishing to break speed records or wreck their bodies would do well to enjoy the hike slowly, taking in its every aspect at a leisurely pace. There is no official record for hiking this trail; the Park Service does not keep records or encourage speed hikes and climbs because of the safety hazards involved. Nevertheless, it is a challenging adventure run for those who enjoy ultra-running in a wilderness setting. Be sure you have adequate support, drink plenty of fluids, and are in proper physical condition for such an adventure.

A trip around the Wonderland Trail can start from any of several points within the park. The most popular starting points are White River Campground and Longmire, although Sunrise, Ipsut Creek and Mowich Lake offer equally easy access. The trail can be hiked in either direction, too, although most travel clockwise around the mountain to avoid the 3½ mi climb from White River to Sunrise. But the climb from White River to Sunrise isn't much better or worse than many of the other ridge climbs along the Wonderland Trail, particularly after many miles of up-and-down hiking.

Preparing for the Wonderland Trail

Wonderland Trail hikers should be well-conditioned and adequately prepared for their trip. This is no trail for the inexperienced. Elevation gain and loss is severe, and much of the trail is in remote areas of the park accessible only on foot. Get in shape by running or walking several miles a few days each week, and by taking long day hikes over varied terrain prior to your trip. Experienced backpackers will know how much and what kind of food, clothing and other equipment to bring with them to make the trip safe and enjoyable. If you haven't undertaken a multi-day backpacking trip before, don't let the Wonderland Trail be your first (just as the summit of Mount Rainier isn't a good choice for your first mountain climbing trip). Plan your trip carefully, be amply prepared for any situation, and know well ahead of time what you are getting yourself into.

You must obtain a wilderness permit and pay a $10.00 fee plus $5.00 per person. Your

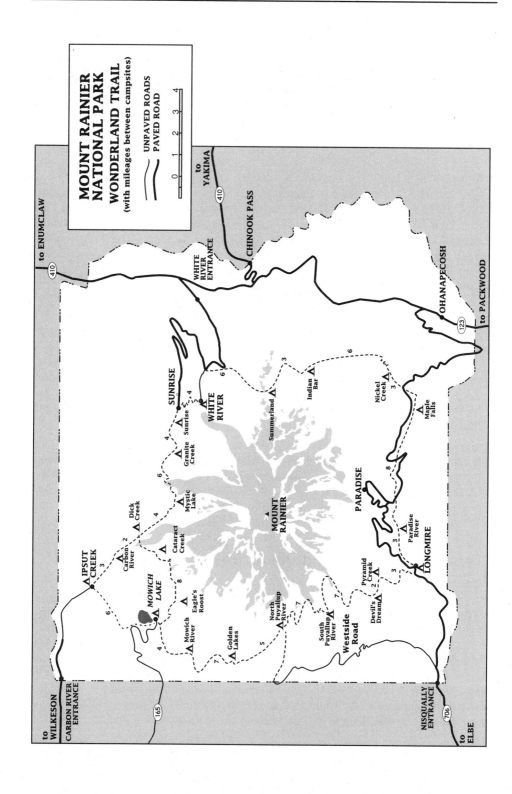

MOUNT RAINIER
NATIONAL PARK
WONDERLAND TRAIL
(with mileages between campsites)

—⌒— UNPAVED ROADS
——— PAVED ROAD

0 1 2 3 4

to ENUMCLAW

to YAKIMA

410

CHINOOK PASS

WHITE
RIVER
ENTRANCE

OHANAPECOSH

123

to PACKWOOD

410

SUNRISE

WHITE
RIVER

Summerland

Indian
Bar

Nickel
Creek

Maple
Falls

6

3

6

3

8

PARADISE

Sunrise

Granite
Creek

4

4

6

Mystic
Lake

Dick
Creek

2

4

Cataract
Creek

Carbon
River

Paradise
River

LONGMIRE

3

3

IPSUT
CREEK

3

8

Eagle's
Roost

MOWICH
LAKE

Pyramid
Creek

2

3

6

Mowich
River

Golden
Lakes

North
Puyallup
River

Devil's
Dream

South
Puyallup
River

Westside
Road

4

7

5

7

7

MOUNT
RAINIER

to
WILKESON

CARBON RIVER
ENTRANCE

165

NISQUALLY
ENTRANCE

706

to
ELBE

permit is good for up to 14 days (you used to stop along the way to renew your permit after seven days). Be aware that you must follow your travel itinerary exactly, staying only at campsites listed on your permit on the nights you said you would stay there. If you change your itinerary, you must get a new permit. Find a roving ranger if you can; he or she may be able to take care of the permit change for you. Otherwise, stop at a ranger station.

Hiking the Trail

A sample narrative of a hike around the Wonderland Trail follows. This description begins from Sunrise (although a majority of hikers begin from Longmire). Parking at a heavy-use area such as Longmire or Sunrise can reduce your exposure to theft and vandalism. All mileages and elevation figures are approximate. Jump in from wherever you wish to begin your journey.

Day 1:

Visit with the ranger and obtain a Backcountry Permit from White River Hiker Information Center. Be sure to ask about trail conditions and campsites. Drive to Sunrise and park and lock your car. Once on the trail, descend steeply 3½ mi to White River Campground. Continue on White River Road and a parallel trail segment to reach Summerland trailhead. Hike to Summerland shelter. Miles: 9¼; Elevation Gain/Loss: +2,100 ft/–2,500 ft.

Day 2:

From Summerland, climb over Panhandle Gap (highest point of Wonderland Trail at 6,800 ft/2073 m), and descend to Indian Bar shelter. A pleasant day's hiking with plenty of time left over for side trips and goat watching. Miles: 5; Elevation Gain/Loss: +800 ft/–1,650 ft.

Day 3:

Descend from Indian Bar along scenic Cowlitz Divide and drop to Nickel Creek, continuing to Box Canyon. Hike to Maple Creek Camp in Stevens Canyon. A long day with lots of downhill hiking. If you have an extra day, stop overnight at Nickel Creek before moving along to Maple Creek. Miles: 10; Elevation Gain/Loss: +1,000 ft/–3,350 ft.

Day 4:

Ascend through Stevens Canyon to Reflection Lakes, then descend to Paradise Valley Camp. Another long day, with mostly gradual uphill hiking. Miles: 9¾; Elevation Gain/Loss: +2,500 ft/–1,250 ft.

Day 5:

Descend along the Nisqually River to Longmire (a good place to pick up supplies). Climb over Rampart Ridge and across Kautz Creek to Devil's Dream Camp. Lots of ups and downs. Miles: 8¾; Elevation Gain/Loss: +2,650 ft/–1,500 ft.

Day 6:

Hike through Indian Henry's Hunting Ground and descend to Tahoma Creek. Continue up over Emerald Ridge and down the other side to South Puyallup Camp. Seems longer than it really is. Miles: 6½; Elevation Gain/Loss: +1,800 ft/–3,000 ft.

Day 7:

Spend a leisurely day climbing to St. Andrews Park and hiking and exploring along the ridge to Klapatche Park. Miles: 4½; Elevation Gain/Loss: +1,800 ft/–300 ft.

Day 8:

Descend to North Puyallup River. Climb through the Silver Fir Forest to Sunset Park and Golden Lakes. Save some time for exploring Sunset Park. Miles: 7½; Elevation Gain/Loss: +1,400 ft/–2,000 ft.

Day 9:

Descend gradually through Sunset Park, then steeply to Mowich River camps. Ascend to Mowich Lake junction, then either to the lake or to Eagle's Roost camp. A long day. If you have more time, stay at Mowich River, then proceed to Eagle's Roost camp the next day. Miles: 11¼; Elevation Gain/Loss: +2,450 ft/–2,350 ft.

Day 10:

From either Mowich Lake or Eagle's Roost camp, ascend to Spray Park and take your time traversing the high parkland. Descend through Seattle Park to Cataract Creek camp. Stay put for the night, or continue to Carbon River camp. Miles: 8½ +/-; Elevation Gain/Loss: +1,900 ft/–3,300 ft. Alternatively, take the "unofficial" segment of the Wonderland Trail over Ipsut Pass and down to Ipsut Creek, then up the Carbon River trail. Either way takes about as long, although the Spray Park variation is more scenic and thus more popular.

Day 11:

Hike at a leisurely pace through scenic Moraine Park to Mystic Lake. Explore and rest up. Miles: 4½; Elevation Gain/Loss: +3,000 ft/–450 ft.

Day 12:

Drop down to cross the West Fork White River at the Winthrop Glacier moraine, and climb to Skyscraper Pass. Hike through Berkeley Park past Frozen Lake to Sunrise. Miles: 8¾; Elevation Gain/Loss: +2,500 ft/–1,800 ft.

By adding or subtracting a few miles each day, you can shorten this trip to as few as 7 days, or lengthen it to 14 days or more. If you are a fast hiker, you can complete the loop in as few as three days, which is much easier if you have support from someone driving to meet you at different locations around the mountain with meals and camping equipment, so you don't have to carry much with you. However, as the author will attest, taking only a few days to hike the entire Wonderland Trail is punishing and not entirely pleasant.

Enjoy the trip at your own pace; if it takes you three years or 30 to finish the Wonderland Trail, so be it. You will be amply rewarded by the experience.

Chapter Six:
Off-Trail Routes

So much has been written about hiking and climbing in Mount Rainier National Park that some visitors either don't know or have forgotten that there are many worthwhile off-trail trips within the park. Many hikers won't venture very far from the trails, and climbers usually have their sights set on Columbia Crest. For those who fall in between, here are a few rewarding passages off the beaten path. Some take way trails to remote lakes or distant summits, others to high meadows and vistas, and some have no trail at all, taking true cross-country and scrambling routes to high meadows, rocky basins and remote summits. Some are easy meadow walks, others are scrambles to prominent peaks, and still a few others are technical rock climbs on frighteningly loose rock. Take your pick, but make sure you are prepared for what awaits you.

Minimize Your Impact

Unfortunately, off-trail hiking is a major source of environmental damage in Mount Rainier National Park, particularly in heavy-use areas near Paradise and Sunrise.

> Off-trail hiking around Paradise and Sunrise is
> against park service regulations and is a citable offense.

To reduce or eliminate potential destruction of high meadows and other sensitive environments within the park, numerous off-trail destinations will be excluded from this guide. Those included here hopefully are distant or obscure enough to avoid trampling by the masses. Some already are too popular and are suffering the effects of their popularity. Those venturing off established trails should take every precaution to minimize their impact. Here are a few recommended practices for off-trail travel within the park:

• Check with park rangers prior to your cross-country outing, to obtain any necessary permits and learn of any special restrictions. Rangers will steer you away from heavily-abused areas, and may be able to provide you with alternative routes that will be better able to absorb your unintentional abuse.

• In remote areas, take your own path whenever possible, rather than following someone else's footsteps. This will help to minimize damage where only a few parties each year might venture.

• Don't hike single file through alpine meadows. Although you might rationalize correctly that by following the same path, you will damage fewer plants, heavy use will destroy plants that otherwise would recover from an occasional footstep. However, a single footstep can destroy heather plants and others.

• If there is already a well-established "dead zone" (i.e., way trail) such as the path leading from the Wonderland Trail to the summit of Skyscraper Mountain, the path from Mowich Lake to Knapsack Pass, or the path to the summit of Plummer Peak, follow it carefully so it doesn't spread – or better yet, go somewhere else and pray it will come back to life. Don't use "social trails" if you can avoid it; go cross-country.

• Walk on snow or rocks whenever possible; stay off plant life, especially in high meadows and alpine zones.

• Don't travel in large parties. Maximum off-trail party size (even for day use) should be five persons, and parties of two or three are recommended to reduce wear on the wilderness. Large parties simply do too much damage.

• Follow the gentlest slope possible. When you tromp down or trudge up steep slopes, your boots dig in and cause serious damage that leads to erosion. Switchback if you can, and tread gently.

• Camping is restricted. Maximum overnight party size for cross-country zones presently is five persons or one immediate family (separate rules for snow camping — see Winter Recreation chapter). Camps must be at least 100 feet from streams and lakes, and should not be on meadows or fragile vegetation. If you don't know which zone you will be camping in, ask a ranger before your trip.

• In cross-country zones, don't use obviously sensitive or heavily-used campsites, and stay only one night at any Wilderness campsite to avoid overuse.

• In alpine zones, use previously used sites, as new sites cannot be constructed, or camp on snow or ice. Don't construct or clear new campsites. The damage can last thousands of years.

• Don't dig into soil, turn over or move rocks or logs. Don't cut trees or other vegetation for any reason. Fires are not permitted.

• Avoid too many trips for water, to lessen erosion of paths to lakes and streams.

• Police your campsite before you leave, to make sure you haven't left a mess.

• Don't mark off-trail routes with plastic tape, cairns or anything else.

Colonnade Ridge (Off-Trail Route #25) and Mount Rainier from Wonderland Trail.
(Photo: Rob Lovitt)

Although many of these routes are little more than hikes without maintained trails, none is recommended for those inexperienced in off-trail wilderness travel, particularly those ascending high on Mount Rainier and those requiring glacier travel, rock scrambling or technical climbing. It is very easy to become lost if you aren't familiar with true wilderness travel, and many of the summits listed below may be reached only by scrambling on rotten, crumbly rock, or by careful routefinding over unmarked mountain terrain. Routefinding skills are very important when you don't have a trail to follow, so don't overestimate your ability. Carry a map and compass and know how to use them. For any snow travel, bring an ice ax and know how to use it; when scrambling on rock, wear a helmet. Be well prepared for poor weather, and allow ample time in case you get caught temporarily off route ("lost," if you aren't afraid to use the word), or out after dark. Don't take shortcuts up blind gullies or over cliffs. Always try to follow the easiest and most obvious route possible, unless it will cause resource damage.

Remember that off-trail travelers face a greater risk of becoming lost, and, if lost, will be more difficult to locate than those who do not stray from established trails. It is a very good idea to let someone know where you will be so you can be located if you get lost or stranded. It is unwise to travel alone in the backcountry, particularly off of established trails. If you do go alone, make sure somebody knows where you are going and when you are expected back.

The following symbols will assist you in determining the level of difficulty you may encounter on these routes:

● No technical climbing required, but previous off-trail experience and routefinding skills will be helpful.

■ Difficult terrain. Possibly Class 2 or 3 scrambling, not recommended for inexperienced scramblers. Routefinding may be difficult. An untimely fall may result in injury, or worse. Getting off route may have serious consequences.

▲ Technical climbing route. Not suitable for any but the most experienced off-trail travelers. Class 3 scrambling and Class 4 and 5 rock climbing and/or glacier travel possible, meaning rope and technical equipment may be necessary. Will require exceptional routefinding skills, and will have a higher objective danger level than is appropriate for inexperienced mountain travelers. Technical climbing and/or glacier experience recommended for all parties.

Routes marked with (12) are hiking trails; those marked with [12] are off-trail routes.

Just a reminder on classifications:

• Class 1 generally is unexposed, easy scrambling, where use of hands is infrequent and there is little risk of serious injury;
• Class 2 is easy scrambling with some exposure, where you could be killed or seriously injured if you fell, but you aren't likely to fall;
• Class 3 is more difficult scrambling with serious exposure, on which some climbers will want the safety of a rope;
• Class 4 is very difficult scrambling where use of a rope is mandatory for all but the foolish and the very experienced;
• Class 5 is technical rock climbing requiring the use of intermediate protection to shorten the length of possible (and sometimes imminent) leader falls.

Some routes may require direct aid: A1 is easy, A2 is harder, A3 harder still, A4 extreme and A5 the ultimate in aid-climbing difficulty.

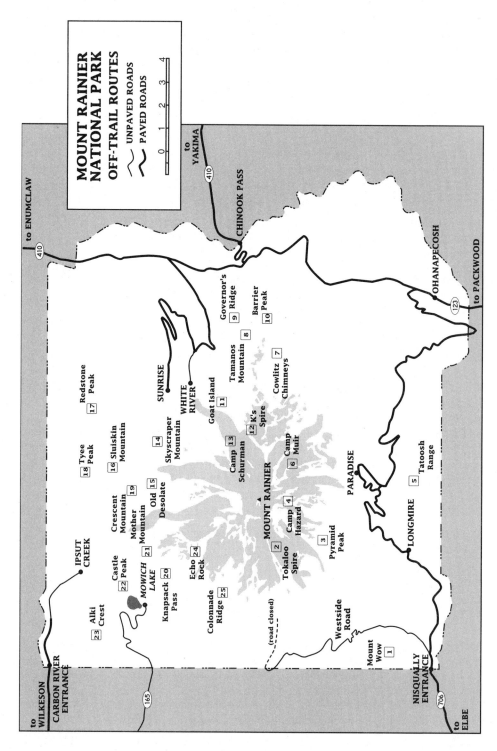

MOUNT RAINIER
NATIONAL PARK
OFF-TRAIL ROUTES

UNPAVED ROADS
PAVED ROADS

0 1 2 3 4

to ENUMCLAW

to YAKIMA

CHINOOK PASS

to PACKWOOD

OHANAPECOSH

Governor's Ridge 9

Barrier Peak 10

Tamanos Mountain 8

Cowlitz Chimneys 7

Redstone Peak 17

SUNRISE

WHITE RIVER

Goat Island 11

Skyscraper Mountain 14

K's Spire 12

Camp Muir 6

Tyee Peak 18

Sluiskin Mountain 16

Camp Schurman 13

PARADISE

Tatoosh Range 5

Crescent Mountain 19

Mother Mountain 21

Old Desolate 15

MOUNT RAINIER

Camp Hazard 4

LONGMIRE

IPSUT CREEK

Castle Peak 22

MOWICH LAKE

Echo Rock 24

Tokaloo Spire 2

Pyramid Peak 3

Alki Crest 23

Knapsack Pass 20

Colonnade Ridge 25

(road closed)

Westside Road

Mount Wow 1

to WILKESON

CARBON RIVER ENTRANCE

NISQUALLY ENTRANCE

to ELBE

410

123

165

706

The Roman numeral grading system used for truly technical routes is as follows: Grades I, II and III denote technical climbs that may take a few hours to much of a day. A Grade IV climb can take all day; Grade V may require a bivouac.

Keep in mind that these designations are very generalized, and are provided only as a rough guide to assist in choosing a route that is appropriate for you – and to keep you off routes that may be too difficult or dangerous for your level of experience. Just because a route is said to be easy doesn't mean it won't be difficult or dangerous for you, especially in poor weather, when snowcovered, or when your experience level is inadequate for the task. Know your limitations, and watch out for your safety. On a maintained trail, you can be reasonably assured that the path won't lead you over the edge of a cliff; when off the trail, you can't be so sure. Proceed with caution. The scrambling and climbing routes contained in this guide are not appropriate for inexperienced scramblers and climbers, unless in the company of an experienced leader. It is best if a member of your party already has done your chosen trip. When the blind lead the blind, parties often end up lost or stranded, or worse. This guide cannot substitute for judgment and personal knowledge gained through experience.

Distances listed in this chapter are approximate only. Remember that cross-country travel takes longer than trail hiking. Cross-country travelers may choose various routes to reach the same destination; therefore, distances and times will vary, and are provided only to give a rough idea of how far and for how long you will be traveling. Time estimates are for a round trip, unless otherwise stated.

Some of these trips are best done from a base at a nearby trailside camp during a two or three-day stay, where you can make several cross-country explorations on a non-hiking day. All are technically possible, if not entirely feasible, as one-day trips for those so inclined.

The following are only some of the hundreds of possible off-trail routes within Mount Rainier National Park. Acres of remote parkland and dozens of minor peaks, ridges and lakes are accessible to those with ambition, off-trail experience, and good routefinding skills. This book will leave out many of these possible excursions so you will have places to explore long after you have traveled the routes included here.

1 Mount Wow ■
Mileage: 4 mi/6 km
Duration: 4 hrs one way from Nisqually Entrance

Mount Wow (6,030 ft/1838 m) occupies a prominent position at the southwest corner of the park. It may be reached via an abandoned boundary trail beginning just inside the park entrance. The trail shows up in older publications and maps, but most who look can't find it. If you are fortunate enough to find the "non-existent" trail (behind the Park Service buildings across from the entrance station), follow it northward to the ridge above Tenas Creek. Climb east to the summit ridge, which leads north to the summit, skirting around a few rocky obstacles.

The standard route is a rough climb from Westside Road to Allen Lake, from which an easy scramble can be made to the summit ridge. The route begins 1⅛ mi from the gate, on the left side, via the barest of cross-country trails. From Allen Lake, scramble to an obvious saddle on the ridge, then go north to the summit (Class 2).

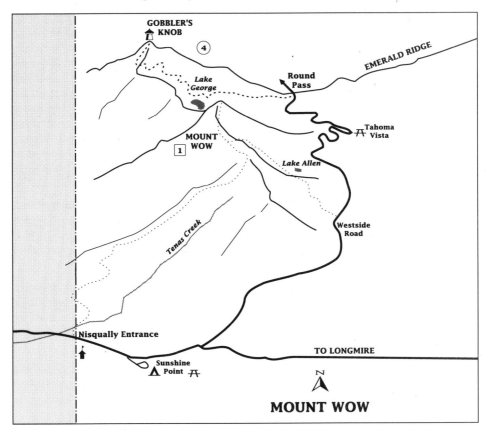

MOUNT WOW

2 Tokaloo Rock and Tokaloo Spire ■ and ▲
Mileage: 3 mi/5 km
Duration: 2 hrs one way from St. Andrews Lake

Tokaloo Rock is situated on Puyallup Cleaver about 1½ mi above St. Andrews Lake. Klapatche Park Trail (Hike 1) offers the shortest access. From the lake, follow the climbers' path east onto Puyallup Cleaver. Continue up the cleaver past Tokaloo Spire to Tokaloo Rock. A Class 2 scrambling route to its summit is obvious.

Tokaloo Spire (7,480 ft/2280 m) is a more difficult objective requiring roped climbing. The route involves a rightward traverse into a wide chimney. This is not a casual climb, and should not be attempted by anyone without rock climbing experience and equipment, including a helmet. Grade I, Class 5.0.

Puyallup Cleaver is a heavy-use area, already suffering from its popularity. Smaller parties help minimize adverse impact. The Park Service intends to implement new limits on overnight use in this area.

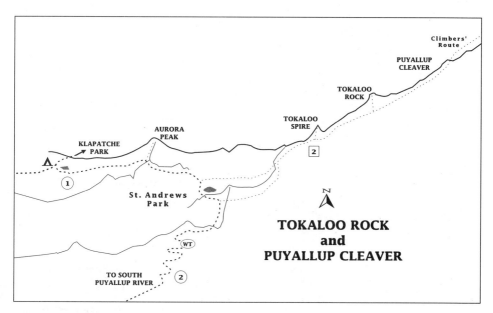

TOKALOO ROCK
and
PUYALLUP CLEAVER

3 Pyramid Peak ●

Mileage: 2 mi/3 km
Duration: 1 hr one way from Mirror Lake

Pyramid Peak is an easy 1 mi ridge hike from the Mirror Lakes Trail's end. Other off-trail trips also begin in the vicinity of Indian Henry's Hunting Ground. Copper Mountain and Iron Mountain commonly are climbed from the pass between them. Satulick Mountain is a short, woodsy excursion south from Devil's Dream Camp. Mount Ararat is an easy (but abused) climb from Kautz Creek Trail. All of these routes are Class 1.

Indian Henry's Hunting Ground and Mirror Lakes are high-use areas, so take extra care to minimize your impact here.

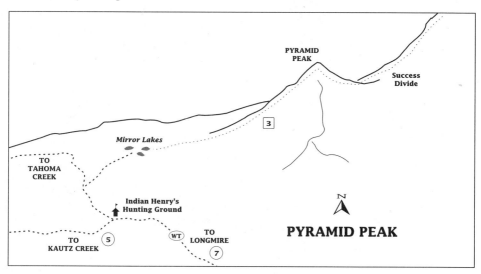

PYRAMID PEAK

4 Camp Hazard
Difficulty: ▲
Mileage: 10 mi/16 km
Duration: 12 hrs from Christine Falls

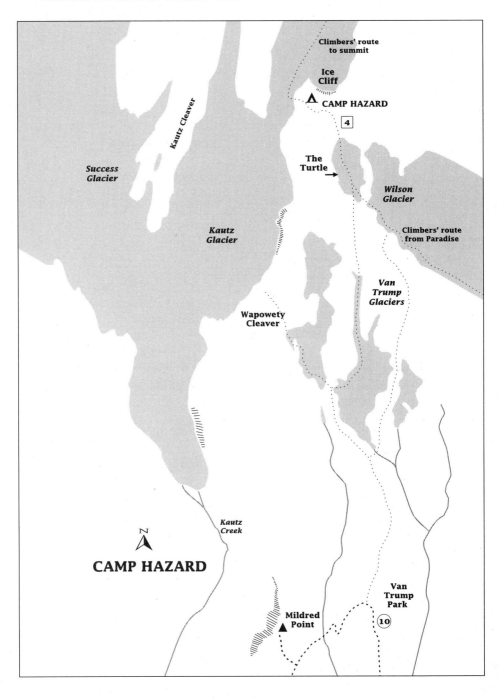

Camp Hazard is situated at about 11,400 feet in elevation on Wapowety Cleaver, and is thus not a casual objective. A climbing permit is required. Camp Hazard may be reached from Van Trump Park without significant glacier travel. This route is best done in late spring, when the trail is mostly clear and snow provides easier travel above Van Trump Park. Earlier trips may have high avalanche danger; later trips may have more difficult terrain. This is a long, strenuous trip high on the mountain; inexperienced mountain travelers should not attempt it. The camp is nothing more than a flat spot on upper Wapowety Cleaver, so don't be disappointed if you arrive there and find nothing but snow, ice, rock and a cold wind coming down from the Kautz Glacier.

Camp Hazard is a heavily-impacted area, with serious human waste disposal problems (i.e., no toilets at Camp Muir or Camp Schurman). Don't make it worse. Travel on snow whenever possible, and use proper waste-disposal methods.

5 Tatoosh Range Traverse ▲
Mileage: 10 mi/16 km
Duration: 10 hrs one way from Longmire to Snow Lake Trailhead

It is possible to traverse the entire Tatoosh Range from Eagle Peak to Stevens Peak, summiting on Chutla Peak, Wahpenayo Peak, Lane Peak, Denman Peak, Plummer Peak, Pinnacle Peak, The Castle, Foss Peak, Unicorn Peak and Stevens Peak along the way. The traverse is equally feasible, beginning from Snow Lake or the Pinnacle-Plummer saddle. Those without scrambling experience can just as easily make the traverse without climbing to the more-difficult summits, which are best left to experienced scramblers. This is not recommended for anyone without off-trail routefinding and scrambling experience, even if you aren't trying the summits. Most of the summits are reached via Class 2 and 3 scrambling. Helmets are recommended due to loose rock and frequent rockfall. Much of this traverse is very heavily used (particularly all areas near hiking trails), so try to minimize your impact. A precise traversing route is not detailed here, to avoid creation of yet another social trail along the crest of the Tatoosh Range. Come when snow allows easier routefinding and less impact, but not so early that avalanche danger negates the advantage. Also, there is extremely high rockfall hazard below Pinnacle Peak and The Castle, as well as near other peaks along the way.

Pinnacle Peak (6,562 ft/2000 m) is the most popular of the Tatoosh Range summits, and can be reached via several routes originating from the Pinnacle Peak Trail (Hike 14). The scrambling route to Pinnacle Peak's summit (Class 2) is not recommended for hikers lacking climbing experience, although adventuresome tourists often try for the top anyway. Class 4 routes are reported on the north and east ridges. Ambitious scramblers often climb The Castle, Lane Peak and Denman Peak, along with Pinnacle and Plummer Peaks, all in one day. All can be reached via Class 2 and 3 scrambling routes. This is a very heavily-abused area; on Plummer Peak, stay on the way trail to avoid further damage. The Mountaineers Trail (page 93) should not be used as the park service is trying to rehabilitate this impacted area.

Unicorn Peak (6,917 ft/2108 m) has a very loose scrambling route (Class 3) on the southwest side, ascending from the saddle above Snow Lake. Off-trail hiking above Snow Lake is particularly hazardous; fatalities have occurred here, so be careful.

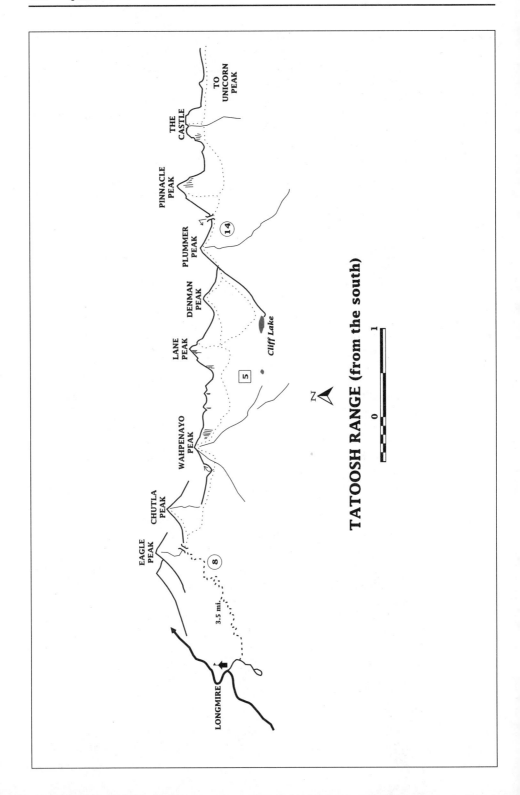

TATOOSH RANGE (from the south)

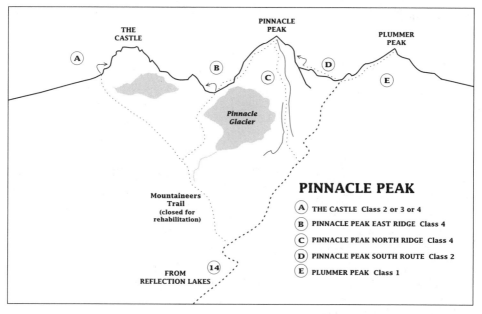

PINNACLE PEAK

- (A) THE CASTLE Class 2 or 3 or 4
- (B) PINNACLE PEAK EAST RIDGE Class 4
- (C) PINNACLE PEAK NORTH RIDGE Class 4
- (D) PINNACLE PEAK SOUTH ROUTE Class 2
- (E) PLUMMER PEAK Class 1

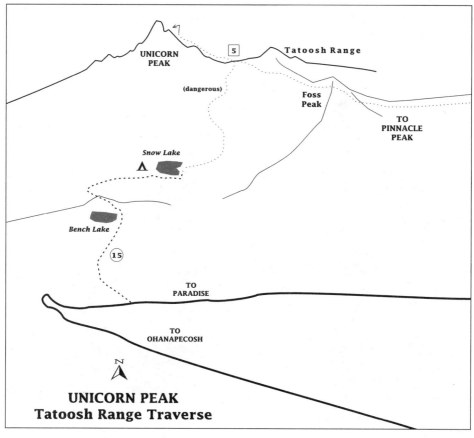

UNICORN PEAK
Tatoosh Range Traverse

6　Camp Muir ▲
Mileage: 10 mi/16 km
Duration: 10-12 hrs

Despite its elevation (10,188 ft/3105 m), or perhaps because of it, Camp Muir is a popular destination from Paradise. Of course, it is the major depot for summit-bound climbers, but hardy hikers and skiers regularly make the ascent. It is a heavily-used area, and will continue to suffer the effects of overuse no matter how conscientious visitors become.

From Paradise, follow the Skyline Trail (Hike 11) to its high point, above Panorama Point. Here a climber's trail continues up along Pebble Creek toward the Muir Snowfield. From here, two routes commonly are used. One contours just above McClure Rock and Sugar Loaf; the other stays on the crest above Panorama Point. Both cross the Muir Snowfield, staying left of the major rock formations (but not too far left), to the gentle saddle below Gibraltar Rock, which is occupied by Camp Muir. Travel on snow whenever possible to minimize impacts. Camping is restricted between Paradise and Camp Muir.

This is not a casual ascent and should not be attempted by those without proper equipment and experience in high mountain travel. Storms and poor weather can leave you stranded with no ability to safely descend. Crevasses sometimes show on the Muir Snowfield in late season (meaning they are hidden earlier in the year, so take care), and avalanches often occur in early season (particularly below Panorama Point and McClure Rock), so this obviously is not a tourist hike. Take crampons and ice axes year round. Take compass bearings on the way up.

An earlier climbing party sets off for the mountain.　(Photo: Natonal Park Service)

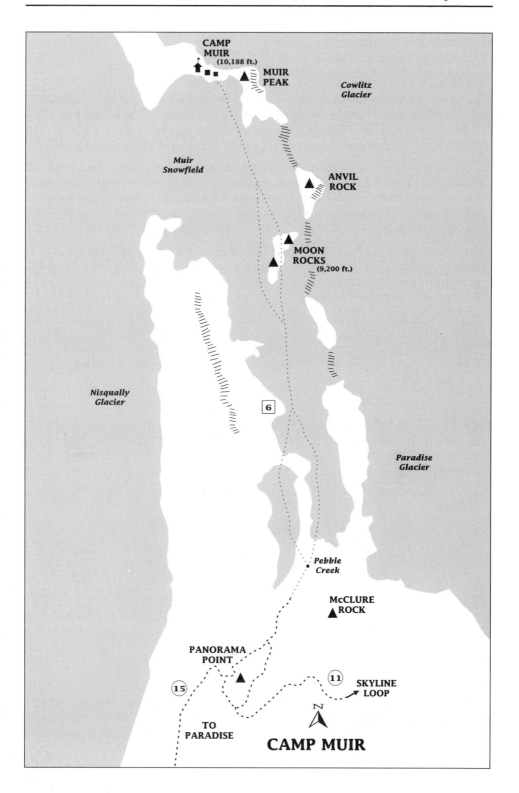

CAMP MUIR

7 Cowlitz Chimneys ▲

Mileage: 7 mi/11.25 km
Duration: 5 hrs from Summerland

The Cowlitz Chimneys are three impressive rock peaks situated on the crest immediately east from Panhandle Gap. The southern chimney is the highest (7,605 ft/2318 m, Class 3), but the middle peak (7,035 ft/2144 m) offers the simplest ascent (Class 2). The northern peak is a technical ascent (Grade I, Class 5) reserved for rock climbers only.

To approach the main and middle peaks, it is easiest to hike from Summerland (Hike 25) to Panhandle Gap, then traverse from Panhandle Gap east across the slopes of Banshee Peak. All three peaks also may be approached from the east, via Owyhigh Lakes or Needle Creek. The approach to the north peak notch is usually made from Owyhigh Lakes Trail (Hike 24).

Although the spectacular views of Mount Rainier and the surrounding landscape may be had from these summits, the views alone are not worth the climb. Except for the middle chimney, the Cowlitz Chimneys are not casual ascents and should not be undertaken by inexperienced scramblers or climbers.

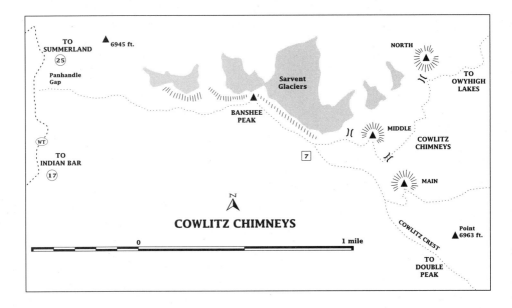

8 Tamanos Mountain ■

Mileage: 8 mi/13 km
Duration: 6 hrs

Tamanos Mountain (6,790 ft/2070 m) is the prominent peak directly west of Owyhigh Lakes. It is reached easily from Owyhigh Lakes Trail (Hike 24) via moderate slopes from near the col between Tamanos Mountain and Barrier Peak. Class 2 scrambling reaches the blocky summit.

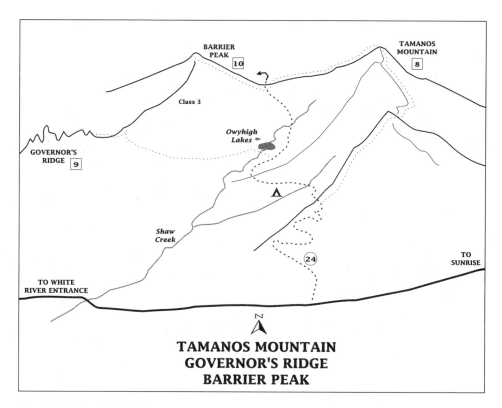

TAMANOS MOUNTAIN
GOVERNOR'S RIDGE
BARRIER PEAK

9 Governors Ridge
Difficulty: ▲
Mileage: 8 mi/13 km
Duration: 8 hrs

Governors Ridge is the spiny crest just east of Owyhigh Lakes, highly visible from Cayuse and Chinook Passes. These rocky summits offer challenging routefinding, with stiff scrambling on poor-quality rock, and are not for inexperienced scramblers, who are better off climbing Tamanos Mountain or Barrier Peak.

The main summit is Governors Peak (6,560 ft/2000+ m), which stands out near the north end of the ridge. There are several ways to reach it: The first is via a long cross-country hike from Cayuse Pass. The second begins from Owyhigh Lakes (Hike 24) via a traverse over the southern saddle and behind (east of) the ridge to the south ridge, or via the northern notch directly from the lakes, up a scree or snow gully, to the north ridge. The southern traverse is Class 3; Class 4 climbing is encountered from the northern notch.

The prominent rock finger near the south end of the ridge is Governors Spire (approx. 6,500 ft/1981 m). There are no published reports that the crumbly spire has actually been climbed. Good luck!

A rope and helmet are recommended for any route on Governors Ridge.

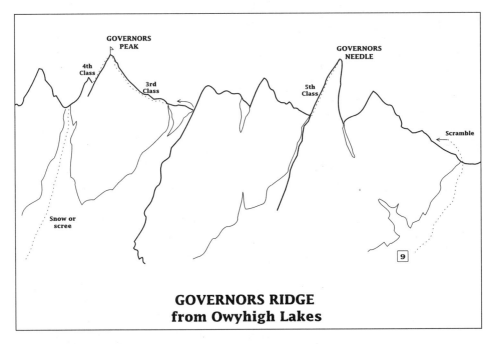

**GOVERNORS RIDGE
from Owyhigh Lakes**

10 Barrier Peak ■
Mileage: 10 mi/16 km
Duration: 8 hrs

Barrier Peak (6,521 ft/1988 m) is the prominent summit at the south end of Governors Ridge. It is most easily reached via Owyhigh Lakes Trail (Hike 24): a short scramble east from the col between Barrier Peak and Tamanos Mountain. The southeast ridge also is a straightforward climb, with easy access from Kotsuck Creek. Buell Peak is ascended easily from the saddle dividing it from Barrier Peak.

11 Goat Island Mountain ■
Mileage: 10 mi/16 km
Duration: 8 hrs

From Summerland (Hike 25), Goat Island Mountain is a fairly easy hike up from the gap dividing it from Little Tahoma Peak; this is a long Class 1 scramble. A steeper route is to ascend an eastern ridge from just beyond the first creek crossing, about 1 mi from White River Road.

12 K's Spire ▲

Mileage: 10 mi/16 km
Duration: 10 hrs from Summerland

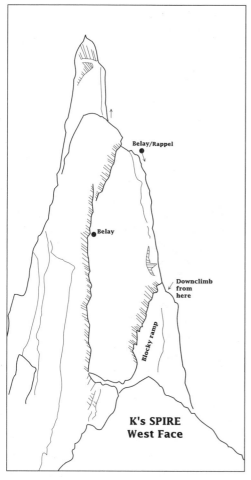

K's SPIRE
West Face

K's Spire (8,886 ft/2709 m) is the prominent gendarme on the lower north ridge of Little Tahoma Peak. It is a technical climb (Grade I, Class 5), which is best approached from Summerland (Hike 25) and Meany Crest by traversing the Fryingpan Glacier.

There are two reported routes: one climbs the south face (said to be mostly Class 4 with a few Class 5 moves); the other up the southwest face (route shown, mostly Class 5). There appear to be other possible routes of Class 5 difficulty. Supplement your rack with a few pitons, and take a helmet. You'll need crampons and ice axes for the glacier traverse, too. Remember, a climbing permit is required for glacier travel.

13 Camp Schurman ▲

Mileage: 10 mi/16 km
Duration: 8 hrs from Glacier Basin

The ascent to Camp Schurman (9,500 ft/2896 m) regularly is undertaken by summit-bound climbers, but for non-climbers the route is different. The climbers' route is more direct, continuing from the end of the Glacier Basin Trail (Hike 26) to the terminus of Inter Glacier, then ascending the glacier to Steamboat Prow (9,700 ft/2957 m). Non-climbers must not ascend the glacier, as it has several deep crevasses. The alternate route is to ascend from Glacier Basin up the northeast shoulder of Mount Ruth via snow or scree (early-season snow gullies offer the most direct and least destructive route), then

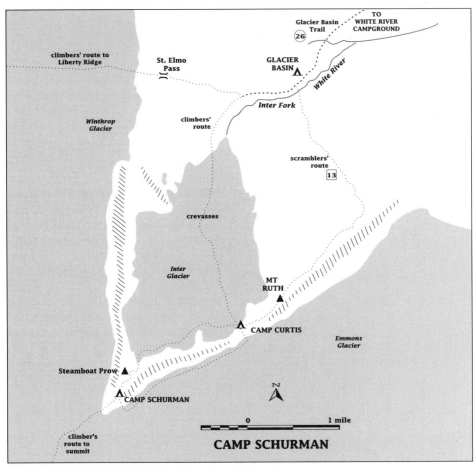

CAMP SCHURMAN

ascend the ridge to its summit (8,501 ft/2591 m) and continue along the left margin of Inter Glacier, which usually is free of crevasses, to Steamboat Prow. From a point just left of Steamboat Prow, descend Class 2 gullies to Camp Schurman.

This is high mountain country, and is subject to increased risks, including rockfall, avalanches and the potential for becoming stranded in poor weather. Prepare accordingly. There are restrictions on how many travelers may stay overnight at Camp Schurman. If you plan on staying overnight, you must obtain a permit. This is a heavily-used area. Climbing on snow can help lessen your impact here.

14 Skyscraper Mountain ●
Mileage: 7½ mi/12 km
Duration: 4 hrs

Skyscraper Mountain (7,078 ft/2157 m) is a prominent summit southwest of Fremont Lookout. It is reached easily via a ¼ mi ridge walk from the Wonderland Trail above Berkeley Park, about 2½ mi west of Sunrise. Take care not to trample any vegetation. The views from the summit are less spectacular than those seen from Burroughs Mountain Trail. Most visitors are just passing through on their way to or from Mystic Lake.

15 Old Desolate, Moriane Park ■

Mileage: 3½ mi/5.5 km
Duration: 4 hrs round trip from Moraine Park

Old Desolate (7,140'/2176m) lies due north of Mystic Lake, and can be reached by scrambling from the Wonderland Trail (Hike 35). The most direct route begins from Moraine Park, climbing a rocky gully to a barren plateau, continuing eastward and scrambling up talus to the top. The true summit lies in the middle of the ridge; points at either end reach to about 7,000' elevation. Traversing the entire ridge is possible, but has some difficult spots (mostly Class1 with occasional Class 2 and 3.)

From the plateau, cross-country hiking northward leads into a secluded section of Moraine Park. Continuing northward over a shoulder of Old Desolate leads through Elysian Fields to Windy Gap. This is fairly rugged and remote going, definitely not for the casual hiker. Also, as this is one of the more unspoiled areas of the park, please tread with care.

Mineral Mountain (6,500'/1981m), a prominent summit rising above Mystic Lake opposite Old Desolate, is easily reached from Moraine Park via scrambling on the southwest side, with close views of Curtis Ridge and Willis Wall. From here it is possible to hike up to the edge of the Carbon Glacier for closer views of formidable Willis Wall.

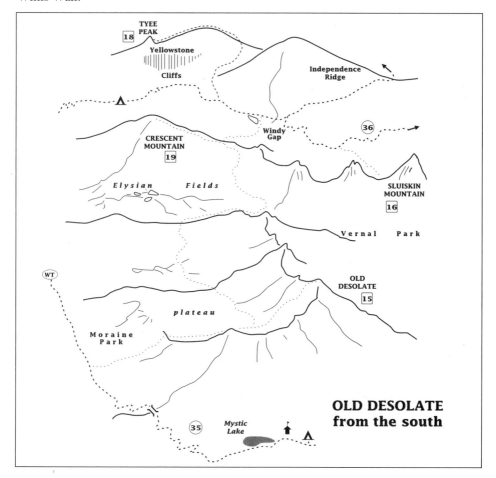

OLD DESOLATE from the south

16 Sluiskin Mountain ■
Mileage: 15 mi/24 km
Duration: 12 hrs from Ipsut Creek

Sluiskin Mountain is a prominent twin peak just southeast of Windy Gap. It has loose scrambling on its two sub-summits, The Chief (the true summit, 6,700 ft/2042+ m) to the east and The Squaw to the west. Either can be climbed from the gap dividing the two, which is attained easily from just east of Windy Gap (Hike 36). These are difficult and exposed scrambling routes (Class 3, though some may want a safety rope for ascent and descent), and not recommended for the inexperienced. The Squaw is the easier of the two. Party-caused rockfall is the greatest hazard here, and helmets are recommended.

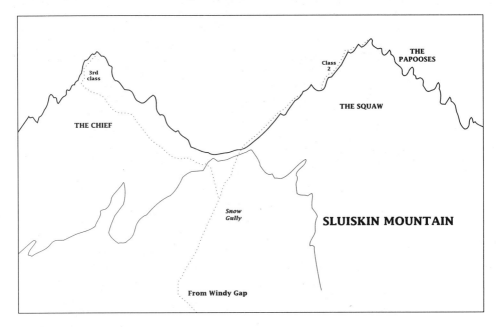

17 Redstone Peak ■
Mileage: 18 mi/29 km
Duration: 2 days

Redstone Peak is just east above Lake James ranger cabin (5,700 ft/1737 m). It is a small rock pyramid on the ridge north of Sluiskin Mountain that offers short scrambling (Class 3) on its north ridge. It is accessed easily by climbing east from the ranger cabin via talus and a wooded, cliffy ridge. The final climb is easier than routefinding up the lower ridge.

18 Tyee Peak ●

Mileage: 14 mi/22 km
Duration: 12 hrs from Ipsut Creek

On maps, Tyee Peak is marked as the small but prominent rock point seen directly above Yellowstone Cliffs from Windy Gap, although the ridge crest immediately east of the rock formation clearly is higher. Either summit is an easy climb from just west of Windy Gap (Hike 36). Skirt Yellowstone Cliffs on the right via a wide basin, climbing gentle slopes to the broad summit area. Those inclined may continue west along the crest to the "summit."

19 Crescent Mountain ●

Mileage: 14 mi/22 km
Duration: 12 hrs from Ipsut Creek

Crescent Mountain, located south across the valley from Tyee Peak, also is an easy climb. Begin the ascent from just west of Windy Gap via a gully (the westernmost of two prominent gullies) and ridge walk. Crescent Lake, nestled below Crescent Mountain, also may be reached from near Windy Pass. The summit is an easy ridge scramble from the lake.

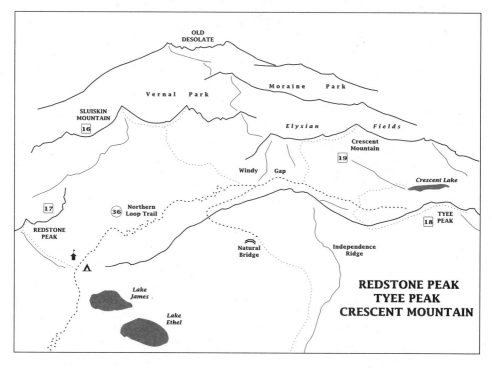

REDSTONE PEAK
TYEE PEAK
CRESCENT MOUNTAIN

20 Knapsack Pass ●
Mileage: 4 mi/6 km
Duration: 3 hrs one way to Mount Pleasant

This is a very popular cross-country hike leading from Mowich Lake to Spray Park. Follow the way trail from the ranger cabin directly to Knapsack Pass. Follow the contours of the slopes and a bench below a rocky shoulder of Fay Peak southward, eventually ascending toward Mount Pleasant. You'll encounter a broad saddle just over Mount Pleasant, from which a social trail descends to Spray Park. From here, you can descend either by trail to Mowich Lake (Hike 38), or wander back over Knapsack Pass. If you descend to Spray Park, don't follow social trails; instead go cross-country and tread gently on the way down.

From the saddle above Spray Park, the usual route up Hessong Rock is on the southwest side, up a gully with a prominent solitary tree at its top (Class 2).

It is easy to ascend from just before Knapsack Pass to Fay Peak (Class 2), then traverse the ridge to Mount Pleasant and Hessong Rock. The ascent of Fay Peak is rocky and enjoyable, but slippery when wet.

The route over Knapsack Pass is very popular, and is suffering the effects of overuse in several places. Do your best to prevent further damage. Early season trips may provide sufficient snowcover to protect plants and lessen erosion. It is recommended that you don't descend to Spray Park, to avoid further damage. As it stands, Spray Park has exceeded the limits of acceptable change mandated by the Wilderness Management Plan.

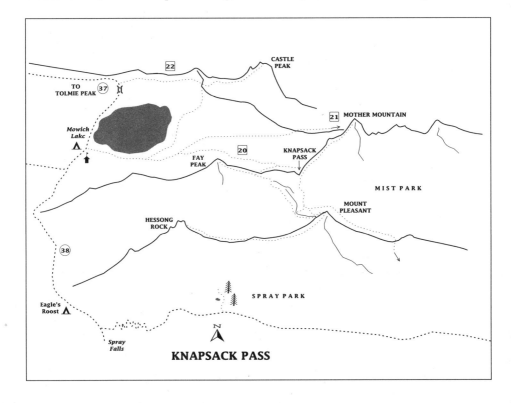

KNAPSACK PASS

21 Mother Mountain ■
Mileage: 3 mi/5 km
Duration: 3 hrs from Mowich Lake

From Knapsack Pass, First Mother Mountain (6,500 ft/1981+ m) is an easy scramble to the east involving some simple routefinding around a few obvious obstacles (Class 2).

Second Mother Mountain commonly is approached from the saddle dividing Mother Mountain and Castle Peak. The route is obvious, following rocky heather slopes directly to the summit (Class 2 or 3).

Third Mother Mountain, the most difficult of the three, may be approached from Ipsut Creek Trail (Hike 33). Routefinding sometimes is harder than the final summit climb, which traverses over the ridge, and climbs a steep face and chimney on the south side to a final, short summit scramble (Class 3).

Second and Third Mother Mountains involve loose, exposed scrambling. Fatalities have occurred here due to loose rock and poor routefinding, so take care. Don't attempt any of

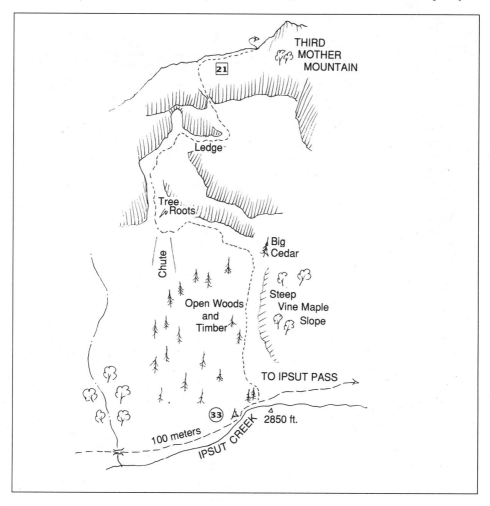

these summits if you aren't very familiar with or prepared for loose scrambling, or when raining or wet. Large parties are discouraged for safety reasons. Helmets should be considered mandatory on these routes.

22 Castle Peak ■

Mileage: 5 mi/8 km
Duration: 4 hrs from Mowich Lake

Although precipitous from three sides, Castle Peak is easily accessible from the southwest. From the Wonderland Trail ½ mi south of Ipsut Pass (Hike 37), traverse the ridge east to a prominent point above Mowich Lake, then northeast across a short sub-ridge to Castle Peak. Alternatively, climb east from the north end of Mowich Lake to the ridge. The summit scramble is exposed but not too difficult (Class 2) if you are on the right route.

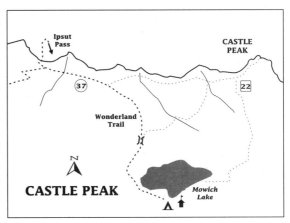

23 Alki Crest ●

Mileage: 6 mi/10 km
Duration: 5 hrs from Mowich Lake

Several minor summits can be reached easily from Tolmie Peak (Hike 37). An easy ridge traverse leads north to Howard Peak (5,683 ft/1732 m). Continue west along the crest to reach Florence Peak. By continuing north from Howard Peak along Rust Ridge, one can reach the summit of Arthur Peak (which also is accessible from Green Lake Trail, Hike 32). Gove Peak is a long ridge hike from just west of Ipsut Pass (or a steep, forested climb from Green Lake Trail, Hike 32).

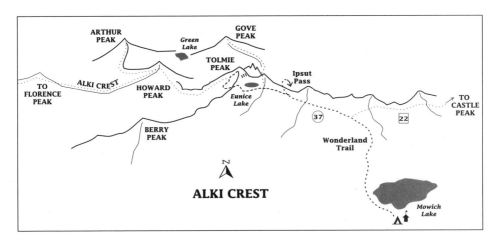

Florence Peak also may be reached by hiking up the old boundary trail from the Carbon River Entrance, then up a wooded ridge to the crest, traveling either over Sweet Peak or around it. The abandoned trail is sketchy due to close-in logging, but shouldn't be too troublesome for experienced off-trail travelers.

24 Observation Rock and Echo Rock ▲
Mileage: 12 mi/19 km
Duration: 10 hrs from Mowich Lake

Observation and Echo Rocks are the prominent peaks at the head (southeast) of Seattle and Spray Parks. They are relatively simple ascents commonly done together.

The shortest route begins from Mowich Lake. Hike to Spray Park (Hike 38). At the trail's highest point (the "divide" between Spray Park and Seattle Park), continue off trail across rolling parkland toward the col between Echo and Observation Rocks. Cross the Flett Glacier, which can be very icy and shows a bergschrund in late season (crampons and ice axe recommended). Both summits can be reached easily from this gap. A short, loose scramble (Class 2/3) on the northwest side reaches the summit of Echo Rock. Observation Rock's southwest side is also easy (Class 1/2); loop around from the glacier.

Those experienced with and prepared for high alpine travel can continue up Ptarmigan Ridge to a prominent point just above 10,000 feet in elevation, but must choose their route carefully to avoid crevasses on the Russell Glacier or on the steep terrain higher on the ridge. Roping up on Russell Glacier is encouraged.

To avoid damage to the high parkland, come early, when snowcover will allow easy travel with minimal impact. Please don't follow social trails through Spray Park.

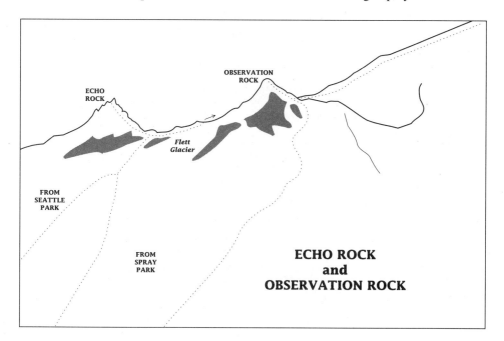

25 Colonnade Ridge
Difficulty: ■
Mileage: 10 mi/16 km
Duration: 8 hrs from Golden Lakes

The Wonderland Trail traverses lower Colonnade Ridge as it contours above Golden Lakes (Hike 39). The ridge crest is reached via an easily-missed trail that begins about one mile south of Golden Lakes ranger cabin on the Wonderland Trail. Continue up the ridge for closer views of Puyallup and South Mowich Glaciers. A prominent rocky point high on the ridge (6,880+ ft) is an obvious destination, although there are several higher points offering closer views. It is possible to continue to the head of the ridge where it cleaves North Mowich and Edmunds Glaciers, but it becomes loose and steep with menacing dropoffs in places.

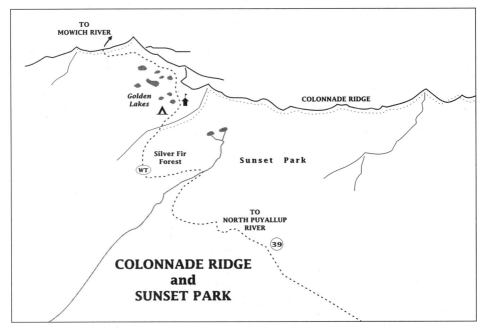

Don't let this guide limit your exploration of this magnificent and remote area of the park. At the same time, try to minimize your impact on this lovely but fragile area.

Chapter Seven:
Summit Routes

More than 4,000 people climb Mount Rainier each year, and almost twice that number attempt it. About 30% of these climbers are guided by Rainier Mountaineering, Inc., the park's sole guide service. Most ascents take the "dog routes" of Disappointment Cleaver and Emmons Glacier (most guided ascents are via Disappointment Cleaver). Often, during a spell of good weather, climbers can follow deep snow trenches (like trails) left by dozens of preceeding parties, all the way to the summit of Mount Rainier. Those seeking a bit more adventure than this should avoid Camp Muir and the above two routes. Alternate routes have dangers and challenges, but are as different to the common routes on Mount Rainier as modern freeways are to abandoned logging roads. Weekend traffic jams on popular routes are common.

A Warning for the Unwary

Because of its prominence and attractiveness to lowlanders, Mount Rainier has been the site of many climbing accidents and fatalities. While thousands of mountain ascents are accomplished safely each year, mountain climbing, and particularly glacier and volcano climbing, have inherent dangers which, although not always obvious, are always present. Many mountain accidents result from inexperienced climbers attempting routes which are too difficult for them or their equipment, or from exercising poor judgment in the face of changing circumstances, and particularly by fatigue-induced error. However, a great many climbing accidents occur by chance, whether due to unforseen avalanches, icefall, rockfall, or other objective hazards, including poor weather. Most climbing accidents are avoidable with the use of good judgment, technique and proper equipment – and a conservative approach to climbing – which can only be developed through experience. In mountain climbing, especially on Mount Rainier, there is no substitute for experience. The routes contained in this guide are no place for unguided, inexperienced climbers. No matter how enticing Mount Rainier appears from below, don't head for the summit, or even onto its glaciers, without prior experience and proper equipment.

If this chapter seems a bit preoccupied with the hazards associated with mountaineering, it is because non-climbers, usually having inadequate experience or equipment, might attempt to climb routes shown in this guide. Non-climbers often head off from Paradise for the summit of Mount Rainier ("It seems so close!"), and even though most turn back before they even reach Camp Muir, the possibility that some may foolishly go on exists. The fact is, there have been fatalities attributable to unprepared and inexperienced climbers attempting to reach Mount Rainier's summit.

Climbing accidents on Mount Rainier historically have involved avalanches, icefall, rockfall, roped and unroped falls down glaciers and into crevasses (individuals and whole rope teams included), hypothermia, mountain sickness and pulmonary edema, among others. Each year, it seems, at least a few people are killed on Mount Rainier. Risk is an inherent part of the summit experience that simply cannot be eliminated. If you are not willing to accept this risk, Mount Rainier is not for you. For those wishing to learn the details of climbing accidents on Mount Rainier, an in-depth accounting is contained in Dee Molenaar's *The Challenge of Rainier*. This information could help you avoid someone else's mistakes.

This is not a climbing instruction guide. If you don't already know how to climb, what equipment to bring, and how to prepare yourself for an ascent of Mount Rainier, you should take a climbing instruction course. For non-climbers reading this book who are inspired to climb Mount Rainier, the author has this to say: Get professional help! There are several guide services authorized to operate on Mount Rainier who are able to assist you to the summit and back, and offer crevasse rescue seminars, high traverses and other programs. They are listed in the Appendix (page 172).

Routes listed in this guide are rated according to difficulty of approach and climbing, committment and exposure to objective hazards. The following system will be used:

● Routes with this symbol do not have much technical or routefinding challenge, but do consist mostly of roped glacier climbing. These are not beginner's routes (no route on Mount Rainier is suitable for inexperienced climbers), but will not be too difficult for climbers with some mountaineering and glacier experience, or those in the company of a guide or experienced leader. You should not expect to encounter unusual objective hazards during optimal conditions. Round trip from high camp to summit will take 6 to 10 hours for most parties.

■ Routes with this symbol are more difficult, and may involve technical climbing and difficult routefinding. Climbers attempting these routes should have ample prior experience in all aspects of mountaineering. Expect increased exposure to objective hazards, including icefall, stonefall and avalanches. Round trip from high camp to summit may take more than 10 hours for competent parties.

▲ Routes with this symbol have high technical difficulty, commitment and routefinding challenge. Also, expect exposure to objective hazards, including icefall, stonefall and avalanches. These routes should not be attempted by any but those very experienced in all aspects of mountaineering. Expect to take at least a full day from high camp to summit and back, and be prepared for a bivouac high on the mountain.

◆ Routes with this symbol are considered "death routes," having an unacceptably high level of objective danger, usually in the form of ice cliffs, loose technical rock climbing, or a high likelihood of rockfall or avalanches. Most climbers know to leave these routes alone. You should, too!

This rating system is very generalized, and does not take any individual route factors into consideration. Also, it is completely invalid during less-than perfect snow, ice and weather conditions. During winter conditions, all routes would be rated at least ▲ on the above scale, although winter conditions sometimes can provide excellent and relatively safe climbing. During late summer, glacier conditions can make even the "easy" routes difficult and dangerous, and very time consuming.

Just a reminder on classifications:

• Class 1 generally is unexposed, easy scrambling, where use of hands is infrequent and there is little risk of serious injury;

• Class 2 is easy scrambling with some exposure, where you could be killed or seriously injured if you fell, but you aren't likely to fall;

• Class 3 is more difficult scrambling with serious exposure, on which some climbers will want the safety of a rope;

• Class 4 is very difficult scrambling where use of a rope is mandatory for all but the foolish and the very experienced;

• Class 5 is technical rock climbing requiring the use of intermediate protection to shorten the length of possible (and sometimes imminent) leader falls.

Some routes may require direct aid: A1 is easy, A2 is harder, A3 harder still, A4 extreme and A5 the ultimate in aid-climbing difficulty.

The Roman numeral grading system used for truly technical routes is as follows: Grades I, II and III denote technical climbs that may take a few hours to much of a day. A Grade IV climb can take all day; Grade V may require a bivouac.

Routes marked with (12) are off-trail/summit routes.

The summit of Mount Rainier. (Photo: Austin Post, U.S.Geological Survey)

The ★ symbol indicates routes that are popular and highly recommended by those who have climbed them.

Estimated climbing times are provided for your reference. These give an average time on the route, usually from high camp to the summit only (unless otherwise stated), and do not include approach or descent times. These are estimates only, and are generous, considering some parties make it from Paradise to the summit and back in a single day, while others take that long from Camp Muir to the summit and back. Plan on at least 4 to 8 hours one-way from high camp to the summit for the easier routes on Mount Rainier. Some routes are more complex, and obviously will take much longer. Your actual time may vary, depending upon your party's experience, fitness and on the conditions you encounter. On routes rated ▲ and ♦, be prepared to bivouac. Even on shorter and easier routes, an unplanned bivouac may be necessary for some parties from time to time. Be prepared for the possibility on all climbs.

Most routes included in this guide can be climbed during a weekend trip, beginning with an approach to high camp Friday evening or Saturday morning, followed by a summit climb very early the following morning, with a quick descent and hike out that day or the next. Begin your summit ascent early so you can descend well before the day's heat softens glacier slopes, which increases the risk of avalanches and stonefall and makes the going much slower. Spend as little time on the summit as possible. The longer you remain at high elevation, the greater your risk.

Standard approach and descent routes will be listed in some detail in this chapter. Listing of an approach or descent in this guide does not mean climbing routes may be approached and descended only by these routes, but only that these are the most commonly used approaches and descents.

Preparing for the Climb

Conditioning can play a major role in climbing safety. You should be in good physical shape before attempting the summit climb, since you will be gaining about 9,000 feet or more in a relatively short distance. Fatigue and sickness quickly lead to injury or death at high elevations. If you get tired, you will slow down your entire climbing party, which will subject not only you but everyone else to increased risk. Train for the climb as you would for a marathon. Running a few miles three or four days a week for two or three months prior to your climb should do it. Learn to run at an even pace for long distances. Climbing to the summit, just as in running, it isn't necessary to go fast so much as to maintain a strong, steady pace. Fatigue is a major contributing factor in many mountaineering accidents. With proper training and conditioning, the likelihood of fatigue-related accidents can be greatly reduced. You should seek your doctor's advice before beginning any exercise program, and if you have any health problems, definitely see your physician before your climb.

Summit Firn Caves

An interesting feature of Mount Rainier is its summit crater firn caves, which are kept open by warm gasses emitted from the volcanic vent ("fumaroles"), a sure sign that the volcano is simply dormant, not extinct. These "steam caves" warmed Stevens and Van Trump in 1870, when they bivouacked on their first ascent. Later parties have sought refuge from storms here. Although tunnel explorations are not recommended, parties with extra time on the summit on nice days sometimes explore a little. Wear a helmet, bring a headlamp, and don't get lost down there!

Climbers who want to pioneer new routes on Mount Rainier will have to settle for minor and usually insignificant variations of existing routes. Although the mountain has many unclimbed features, all of its faces, ridges and glaciers have been climbed by at least one route, and usually several distinct routes. Most unclimbed lines were left unclimbed for a reason, either due to loose rock or extreme objective danger. Although you need not limit yourself to the routes already done or listed in this guide, you should plan any first ascent on Mount Rainier with safety as your first consideration.

Fixed equipment on Mount Rainier, such as bolts and ladders crossing crevasses, etc., have been put in place from time to time, but this practice may end at the Park Service's direction. For example, RMI has put ladders across crevasses on its guided routes in past years, but the practice may not be allowed to continue. If you use equipment already in place, do so at your peril.

Recommended Climbing Practices and Equipment

The Park Service recommends the following climbing practices for all parties:

• Conditioning climbs on similar glaciated peaks and participation in mountaineering schools are good builders of experience and judgment. Rescue and first-aid training are essential.
• The climb leader should have first-hand knowledge of the ascent and descent routes and be responsible for his/her team and their climbing practices.
• Climbers should remain roped together on all glaciers and crevassed snowfields.
• Climbing teams should consist of at least three people and be adequate to effect a rescue or go for help. For winter ascents, a minimum party of four people is recommended.

The Park Service recommends the following equipment for all summit climbers:

• Full-frame crampons	• Ice axe
• Lug-soled boots	• Sunglasses/goggles
• Wool clothing	• First-aid kit
• Down clothing	• Sunblock
• Waterproof clothing	• Food
• Hard hat	• Carabiners (2)
• Rope (7/16 inch x 120 feet)	• Sleeping bag
• Mittens and gloves	• Prusik slings (3) or
• Ensolite pad	• Ascenders (2)
• Flashlight	• Headlamp
• Map and compass	• Pitons, ice screws
• Rescue pulleys	• Stove and fuel
• Wands	• Tent

The park service recommends you bring the following additional equipment for winter ascents:

• Extreme cold sleeping bag	• Down parka, pants, mitts
• Double boots	• Snowshoes or skis
• Expedition tent	• Snow shovel
• Extra wands (200 minimum)	• Extra food and fuel (2 days)
• Two-way radio	• Altimeter
• Avalanche cords or beacons	• Avalanche probes
• Additional ropes	

Human impact on Mount Rainier has been tremendous during recent years, especially at Camp Muir and Camp Schurman. Litter and human waste are the main problems. Please use toilets for waste elimination only, and not for litter disposal. Pack out whatever you bring with you. If you can't use a toilet, pack your waste out using the Park Service's blue bags (available from rangers). Use existing campsites, and camp on snow or ice whenever possible to minimize your impact in Mount Rainier's alpine zones. The Park Service intends to begin eliminating unnecessary and unauthorized alpine-zone campsites, and will designate only a few sites for overnight use. Group-size limits for alpine zone camping are: 5 persons on bare ground sites; parties of 6 to 12 on permanent snow.

Climbing Permits and Fees

Climbers must obtain a permit and pay a $15.00 fee to climb Mount Rainier or ascend to high camps. A $25.00 annual pass is available for those who plan on climbing the mountain more than once per season.

Climbers going higher than 10,000 feet, traveling off trail, or camping on glaciers are required to register and obtain permits in advance, and to check out upon their return. The park service limits the number of people occupying popular campsites, such as Camp Muir and Camp Schurman, and permits are issued on a first-come, first-served basis (no reservations accepted). Party size is limited to 12 persons. Climbers under the age of 18 years must have written parental consent. Parties of two or more are required above high camps. Solo climbers must obtain advance written permission from the park superintendent. Guiding for a fee is prohibited, except for the authorized concessions. Any violation of these regulations is a federal offense.

Check weather, avalanche and route conditions before your climb. If in doubt, or facing uncertain weather, it is better to turn back before you reach a point of no return.

Climbing conditions are reported on the Mount Rainier National Park homepage, **www.nps.gov/mora/climb_cd.htm**. The climbing conditions report is updated by the climbing rangers as conditions change or as significant reports come in from the mountain.

In the event of an emergency, call 911, or contact the park service at (360) 569-2211. For further information about climbing Mount Rainier, contact Mount Rainier National Park, Tahoma Woods, Star Route, Ashford, WA 98304, (360) 569-2211.

Camp Muir Approach

Most routes on Mount Rainier's east side are approached via Camp Muir, which is reached from Paradise (Off-Trail Route 7) These routes include Nisqually Icefall and Ice Cliff, Gibraltar Ledge and the Ingraham Glacier route. Camp Muir was named for John Muir, who, recognizing the presence of light pumice on the ground as an indication of shelter from wind, selected the site during his 1888 ascent of the mountain. Camp Muir is typically overcrowded. The park service permits only 100 people per night at Camp Muir, and reservations are not accepted. It has a public shelter available on a first-come, first-in basis, plus rock windbreaks for tents. Toilet facilities are in place here – use them!

Camp Muir summit routes. (Photo: Austin Post, U.S.Geological Survey)

1 Gibraltar Ledge ■
Duration: 4-6 hrs
Rating: II, Class 4

Gibraltar Ledge was the route most used in early ascents of Mount Rainier, and was very popular until 1936, when a large portion of the ledge fell away. The route was not climbed again until 1948, and has only recently regained some of its former popularity. It is a dangerous route, subject to random rockfall, and is not recommended.

From Camp Muir, climb the glacier past the "Beehive" (a prominent rock tower on Cowlitz Cleaver) and along the left flank of Gibraltar Rock. Traverse the wide ledge to a rappel (anchor in situ for now) or downclimb (not recommended) that reaches a lower ledge system. (A rope already may be in place for your return to the upper ledge system; if not, you should consider leaving one in case you aren't up to climbing back to the ledge. Just don't leave it as a permanent fixture.) Traverse across the lower ledges to where ice ramps and gullies lead back to the upper ledge. Steep slopes reach the head of Gibraltar Rock (elevation 12,660 feet). Continue up the glacier to the crater as crevasses permit, then across to the summit.

Early season ascents are easier, as snow covers the somewhat unstable rock. Expect to take at least 8 hrs round trip from Camp Muir. Ascend very early so you can avoid being pelted by rocks or large icicles on your descent. Helmets are highly recommended.

2 Disappointment Cleaver – Ingraham Glacier ●
Duration: 4-6 hrs

The Disappointment Cleaver ("D.C.") route presently is the most frequently-traveled route on Mount Rainier. More than half of all annual ascents are made by this route, as it is the usual route guided by RMI.

From Camp Muir, there are two primary variations. The Cadaver Gap variation climbs the Cowlitz Glacier beneath Gibraltar Rock and passes through the namesake gap to reach the Ingraham Glacier headwall. Continue up the steep glacier to the head of Gibraltar Rock, and to the summit. This version subjects climbers to rockfall from Gibraltar Rock.

The customary route traverses the Cowlitz Glacier to Cathedral Gap (the first passable gap below Cadaver Gap). From the gap, continue across the Ingraham Glacier as crevasses permit to reach Disappointment Cleaver. Ascend the left flank of the cleaver (snow early season, loose rock later). Continue up the upper Ingraham Glacier to the east crater, then across to the summit. This route has icefall hazard below Disappointment Cleaver, and some rockfall from the cleaver. Parties should move fast to avoid prolonged exposure to these dangers. Helmets should be handy.

Camp Schurman Approach

Camp Schurman is situated at 9,500 feet, at the head of Steamboat Prow where it cleaves the Emmons and Winthrop Glaciers. The Emmons Glacier and Russell Cliff routes begin from here. The park service permits only 35 climbers per night at Camp Schurman (which includes Emmons Flats). Reservations are not accepted. Camp Schurman has a climbers' hut (for emergency use only) equipped with a radio; the camp also has toilets (use them!) and a number of rock windbreaks and existing campsites. High winds have stolen more than one tent here. Many climbers prefer to camp about 300–500 feet above Camp Schurman on the glacier (Emmons Flats) to get an earlier start and avoid the crowds below.

Approach Camp Schurman via White River Campground and the Glacier Basin Trail (Hike 26). From trail's end, continue up a climbers' path to the terminus of the Inter Glacier. Ascend the glacier (rope up, there are crevasses) obliquely left to the gap between Mount Ruth and Steamboat Prow, the site of formerly popular Camp Curtis. From here, either descend to the Emmons Glacier and along Steamboat Prow to Camp Schurman, or continue to a point just left of the summit of Steamboat Prow, and descend the most feasible looking gullies to Camp Schurman, elevation 9,500' (Off-Trail Route 13).

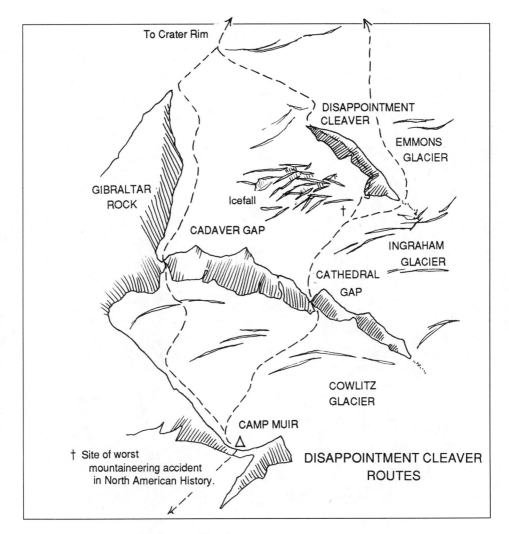

To Crater Rim

DISAPPOINTMENT
CLEAVER

EMMONS
GLACIER

GIBRALTAR
ROCK

Icefall

CADAVER GAP

†

INGRAHAM
GLACIER

CATHEDRAL
GAP

COWLITZ
GLACIER

CAMP MUIR

† Site of worst
mountaineering accident
in North American History.

DISAPPOINTMENT CLEAVER
ROUTES

3 Emmons – Winthrop Glacier ● ★
Duration: 4-6 hrs

This route probably was ascended in 1855, definitely in 1884. It presently is the second most popular route on Mount Rainier.

From Camp Schurman, ascend left and up on the Emmons Glacier to "The Corridor," a usually unbroken pathway between crevasses that ends about halfway to the summit. Continue up the glacier as crevasses permit. The final obstacle, the bergschrund, usually may be passed on either end.

There are few appreciable dangers on this route, other than those normally encountered on long glacier climbs (e.g., crevasses, icefall, avalanches).

Mount Rainier and Little Tahoma Peak. (Photo: Austin Post, U.S.Geological Survey)

4 Winthrop Glacier – Russell Cliff ▲
Duration: 6-8 hrs
Rating: III, Class 4 or 5 possible

In September 1989, a massive rockfall occured from Russell Cliff, scattering an estimated 2.6 million cubic yards of debris across the lower half of the Winthrop Glacier. Because of this, the condition of this route is not known. However, the rockfall does not appear to have affected the Russell Cliff routes.

The original version of this route traverses from Camp Schurman across the Winthrop Glacier toward the cliff. A steep snow-ice traverse above Russell Cliff leads to ice gullies that pass through the cliff's rock bands to Curtis Ridge.

The later version traversed from Camp Schurman up a snow and ice bowl near the top of Russell Cliff. Steep ice leads to rock bands, which may be passed via loose rock or steep ice by a number of possible routes. Continue over Curtis Ridge to the summit.

Descend via the Winthrop-Emmons Glacier route to Camp Schurman. Difficult ice, steep snow and loose rock may be encountered on either variation. Ice screws, pitons and helmets are suggested.

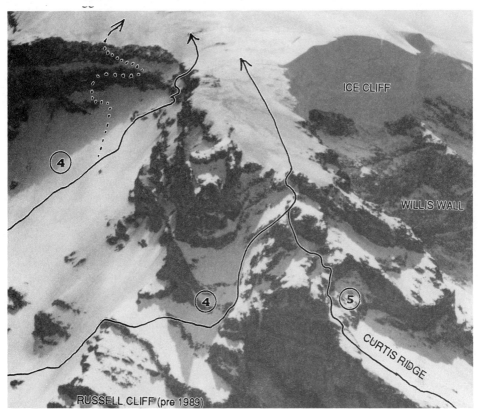

Routes from Russell Cliff. (Photo: Austin Post, U.S.Geological Survey)

St. Elmo Pass Approach

St. Elmo Pass is the saddle dividing The Wedge (Steamboat Prow) from Burroughs Mountain, and is the usual route taken to reach Curtis Ridge and upper Carbon Glacier routes, including Willis Wall and Liberty Ridge. Approach via White River Campground and the Glacier Basin Trail (Hike 26). From trail's end, scramble over St. Elmo Pass and cross the Winthrop Glacier. In late season, this may not be feasible due to the rockfall debris on the glacier – but nobody in their right mind should be on Curtis Ridge or Willis Wall in late season! In early season, snowcover should prevent any problems of this sort. Many parties using this approach bivouac on lower Curtis Ridge.

5 Curtis Ridge ◆
Duration: 12 hrs minimum
Rating: V, Class 5 or aid

Like Russell Cliff, the condition of this route is not known due to the recent rockfall. It appears that much of the route survived intact. Climbers should beware of future rockfall and unstable rock, especially on the eastern flank of the ridge. The route has been moderately popular as one of the most technical on Mount Rainier, despite its reputation as a "suicide ridge." When well frozen, this is said to be a fine technical route.

Cross over from St. Elmo Pass. Once on Curtis Ridge, ascend snow slopes and the narrowing ridge past a prominent gendarme (on the east/left), rappelling over at least one cliff, to reach a notch, from where the real difficulties begin.

The route has several reported variations, involving possible direct aid, water ice, loose Class 5 climbing, and direct stonefall. Most parties skirt the first cliff bands to the right via ice slopes and loose rock. Routes ascending the rock band directly will involve direct aid on loose rock. Once above the first rock band, the route follows snow and ice slopes and gullies, weaving through the rock bands (or over them, on occasional variations). The final rock band has an ice gully, allowing easier passage to the upper ridge.

It is best to climb this route after several cold days with a moderate snow pack, and early in the day, when rocks are frozen in place or embedded in snow. Parties moving too slowly on this route should consider retreat, especially if rockfall becomes a problem. There has been a fatality here due to rockfall. Helmets are highly recommended. Bring pitons and ice screws. Expect to take much of the day to climb the technical portion of the ridge. Stay on snow and ice as much as possible, and move fast!

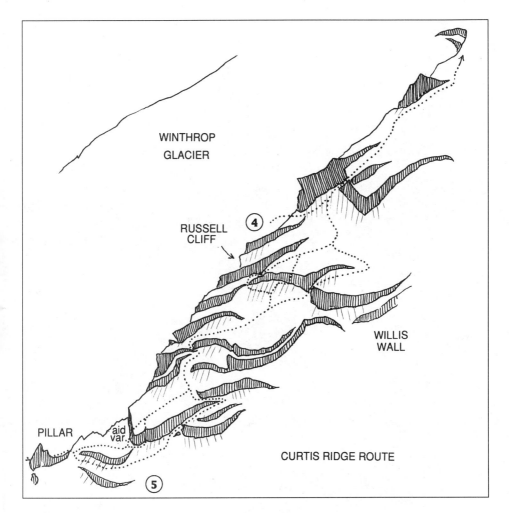

Willis Wall

Of the north faces in North America, Mount Rainier's Willis Wall is one of the most infamous, and assuredly is the most appalling. Rising nearly 4,000 feet above the Carbon Glacier, Willis Wall is a dark, foreboding depression of loose rock that regularly is scoured by immense ice avalanches from the 300-foot-high ice cliffs hanging over the wall. Considering the poor quality rock, the technical nature of the climbing, and the constant threat of bombardment from rock and icefall, routes on Willis Wall are among the most hazardous anywhere in the world. Surprisingly, there have been no reported fatalities on Willis Wall; this is more likely due to the small number of climbers who have climbed or attempted it, and the collective wisdom and experience of those who have climbed it or known better.

Routes up the Willis Wall. (Photo: Austin Post, U.S.Geological Survey)

Willis Wall was named for Bailey Willis, a noted geologist who made early explorations of the northern side of Mount Rainier. Perhaps, however, Willis would have prefered not to be remembered by the most-fearsome feature of the mountain. The wall was first ascended in 1961 by Charles Bell, solo, in a disputed effort that has since come into wider acceptance.

All routes on Willis Wall have considerable rock and icefall danger, in addition to the usual hazards of mountaineering. You might think the buttresses offer protection from ice avalanches, but they really don't. If you watch the face for any length of time, you will see that avalanches frequently spill over the buttresses and would easily wipe out any climbing party on the face. Rocks regularly tumble down the face, particularly during periods of thawing, and large rockfalls have been noted in the past.

The best conditions for an ascent of Willis Wall are usually found during early season, when snow still coats the face, and immediately after several consecutive cold days, which ensures loose rocks are stuck in place and some rock sections will be covered by snow. Favorable conditions can occur throughout the year, although even the most favorable conditions will not guarantee success or survival on Willis Wall. While ascending immediately after an ice avalanche would seem to offer security, there is no guarantee that another ice avalanche will not happen. Winter ascents have been made, although it is difficult to find enough climbing days between storms to make the ascent. Be prepared to bivouac on any ascent of Willis Wall, but try to avoid a bivouac on the wall by any means possible.

Because of the difficult technical nature and extreme objective danger of all reported routes on Willis Wall, none is at all recommended. Helmets, pitons, ice screws and a four-leaf clover are suggested for all Willis Wall routes.

Willis Wall may be approached either from St. Elmo Pass or Moraine Park.

6 Willis Wall – East Route ◆
Duration: 12 hrs minimum
Rating: V, Class 5

This route begins on the far left side of Carbon Glacier and ascends towards lower Curtis Ridge before working back right on the left margin of Willis Wall. It has serious rock and icefall danger. Several rock pitches ascend very dubious rock.

7 Willis Wall – East Rib ◆
Duration: 12 hrs minimum
Rating: V, Class 5

This route climbs the buttress that rises across the wide gully immediately right of the start of the East Route, and finishes at or near Liberty Cap. This route also has some dubious rock pitches, and serious rock and icefall danger.

8 Willis Wall – Central Rib ◆
Duration: 12 hrs minimum
Rating: V, Class 5

This route climbs the central buttress of Willis Wall, which is said to offer some protection from icefall, but not much. There are some technical rock pitches passing rock bands. The route has serious rock and icefall danger.

9 Willis Wall – West Rib (Brumal Buttress) ◆
Duration: 12 hrs minimum
Rating: V, difficult Class 5

This route was used for the first ascent of Willis Wall. It climbs a major buttress, which fades out near the top. Like all the other Willis Wall routes, this route has serious rock and icefall danger.

10 Willis Wall – "Thermogenesis" ♦
Duration: 6-8 hrs on wall
Rating: III, Class 3

This route ascends the "suicide gully" immediately right of the central rib. It has extreme icefall danger, perhaps more so than any other route in this guide, because it climbs a main ice avalanche gully. There is some scrambling through rock bands, which may occasionally include rockfall. If it wasn't for the ice cliff avalanches, this might be the safest route up Willis Wall; it is certainly the fastest when conditions are good.

Moraine Park Approach

Some parties approach Willis Wall and Liberty Ridge via Moraine Park, although this is a bit longer than crossing St. Elmo Pass. Begin from Ipsut Creek Campground and hike the Wonderland Trail (Hike 35) into Moraine Park. From just below the saddle (where the trail drops to Mystic Lake), continue cross country through Moraine Park to a bivouac site above the upper Carbon Glacier (some stone windbreaks exist here — don't build any more!). From here, the glacier is easily accessible.

11 Liberty Ridge ▲ ★
Duration: 10-12 hrs on ridge
Rating: V, Class 4

Liberty Ridge easily is the most popular north face route on Mount Rainier. It is included in *Fifty Classic Climbs of North America,* which has no doubt added to its popularity. First ascended by Jim Borrow, Arnie Campbell and Ome Daiber in 1935, it was not repeated for 20 years.

The usual approach is via St. Elmo Pass, then across Curtis Ridge and the Carbon Glacier to the toe of Liberty Ridge. This approach is best done in early season, before crevasses on Carbon Glacier become difficult. Alternatively, approach via Moraine Park and bivouac just above the glacier, then cross the glacier to the toe of the ridge, as crevasses permit. A late-season bergschrund can block access.

From the toe of the ridge, ascend the snow-ice slopes right of the ridge crest, crossing over rock ribs or along the ridge crest in places, to "Thumb Rock" at about 11,000 feet (usual bivouac site). Continue right up an ice gully or farther right via open ice slopes to the top of the final rocks ("Black Pyramid") and the Liberty Cap Glacier. Continue to Liberty Cap. The most difficult portion of the route often is passing the bergschrund at about 13,000 feet; this can vary each year from steep snow to one or two pitches of steep ice.

This route is long and more serious than many parties anticipate. Perhaps due to its "classic" status, it has lured many an unsuspecting climber to his demise. This route has rockfall danger, and can have serious avalanche conditions after fresh snowfall. Take ice screws and helmets.

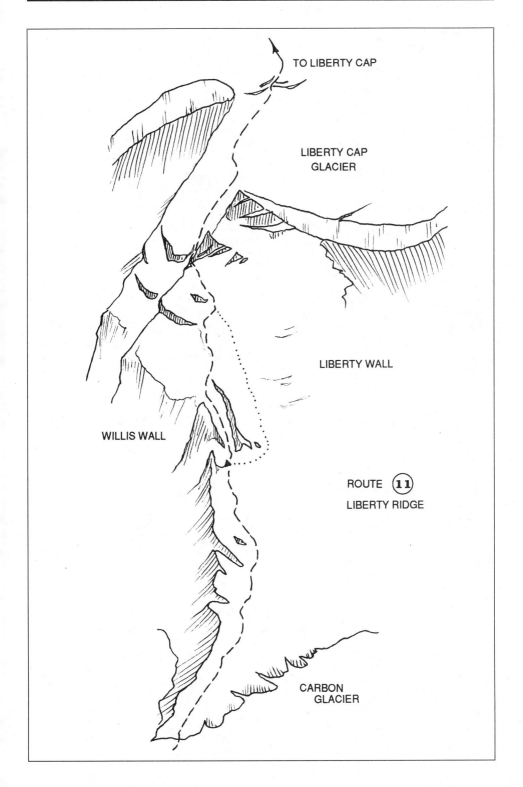

TO LIBERTY CAP

LIBERTY CAP
GLACIER

LIBERTY WALL

WILLIS WALL

ROUTE ⑪
LIBERTY RIDGE

CARBON
GLACIER

12 Liberty Wall ◆
Duration: 10-12 hrs on wall
Rating: IV, Class 4 or 5

This route climbs the headwall immediately right of Liberty Ridge, and passes through the Liberty Cap Glacier ice cliff. Two variations have been reported.

Approach via Russell Glacier from Mowich Lake and Spray Park (Hike 38; see Ptarmigan Ridge approach for details), or from Moraine Park, crossing the Carbon Glacier (as for Liberty Ridge). Drop down from the Russell Glacier into the cirque at the base of the headwall. Ascend either variation at your peril (ice cliffs, rockfall, threat of imminent death from above on both). If the ice cliff on the left route is impassable, it is possible to escape via Liberty Ridge.

Both variations are objectively dangerous, and all warnings that apply to Willis Wall apply here. Bring ice screws, pitons and a helmet, and cross your fingers.

Spray Park Approach

Parties climbing Ptarmigan Ridge almost always use this approach; some parties climbing Liberty Ridge and Liberty Wall approach this way also. From Mowich Lake, hike into Spray Park (Hike 38). Leave the trail at its high point and hike cross-country to the gap between Echo Rock and Observation Rock (Off-Trail Route 24) to reach the Russell Glacier. Those climbing Ptarmigan Ridge will continue on Russell Glacier just below the crest of Ptarmigan Ridge to a bivouac site at the notch just beyond Point 10,310. Others will drop down Russell Glacier to Carbon Glacier and the base of Liberty Wall. Russell Glacier is crevassed, so rope up!

Spray Park is suffering from overuse, so try to minimize your impact while passing through the parkland. Hike on snow whenever possible. Don't leave the trail if you don't have to do so.

13 Ptarmigan Ridge ▲ ★
Duration: 12 hrs minimum
Rating: IV, Class 4

This route is one of the finest on Mount Rainier, considering all factors including alpine nature, continuity of line, committment and difficulty. It was first ascended by Wolf Bauer and Jack Hossack in 1935.

The original ascent climbed ice slopes and ledges more or less directly above the bivouac site, with attendant rockfall hazard and difficult (for 1935) ice climbing.

The second ascent party found an easier way. From camp, drop onto the North Mowich Glacier and traverse beneath the rock buttress to a prominent snow-ice corridor leading leftward between the rock bands. Ascend continuous snow and ice slopes to a final rock buttress, then exit left up an ice chute to the Liberty Cap Glacier. Continue to Liberty Cap.

Another variation ascends left from the notch and skirts the Liberty Cap Glacier ice cliff, then ascends the glacier above to Liberty Cap. This variation is more direct, but much more dangerous than the standard route.

The most recent variation of this route climbs directly over the imposing ice cliff via a fracture on the right side. When the cliff is "in shape," two or three pitches of steep (70 degree) ice are the norm. Definitely not for the squeamish! Bring plenty of ice screws if you dare even try it. Not at all recommended.

This route is quite committing and difficult. It should not be attempted except during periods when loose rock is likely held in place by snow and ice. The ice cliff variations have the additional hazard of icefall. Descents are usually made via another route (Emmons Glacier, Tahoma Glacier, Furher Finger, Liberty Ridge). Bring ice screws and helmets.

Mowich Face

Mowich Face is the steep wall below Liberty Cap on the west, between Ptarmigan and Sunset Ridges. The wall is consistently steep (40 to 50 degrees), and like Willis Wall, has hanging ice cliffs and a propensity for stonefall, though not in the same degree. Hanging glaciers on the face feed the North Mowich and Edmunds Glaciers, which abut the wall at just above 9,600 feet. The face narrows to a shoulder of Liberty Cap at about 13,600 feet.

Routes on Mowich Face commonly are approached via Klapatche Park (Hike 1). From St. Andrews Lake, a climber's trail leads up Puyallup Cleaver to a traverse of the Puyallup and South Mowich Glaciers, which leads onto the Edmunds or North Mowich Glaciers. Some parties have approached via Colonnade Ridge from Sunset Park (Hike 38 and Off-Trail Route 25); however, this is longer than most modern climbers care to walk on the approach. Bivouacs customarily are made on the several rock ridges and nunataks (islands of rock jutting through glacial ice) immediately below the face. Descents usually are made via the Tahoma Glacier route or Sickle variation after a summit stop atop Liberty Cap. Those who continue to Columbia Crest often descend to Camp Muir or via Furher Finger to Paradise.

All routes on Mowich Face should be attempted only during periods of snow and rock stability, as recommended for Willis Wall and Curtis Ridge. The period between mid-June and mid-July has been suggested theoretically as the best to attempt the ascent. Hanging ice and loose rock climbing contribute to this face's difficulty and danger. Ice screws, pitons and helmets are suggested.

14 Mowich Face – North Mowich Glacier Icefall ▲
Duration: 12 hrs minimum
Rating: V, difficult Class 5 or aid

This route skirts around the leftmost headwall by climbing on or beside the steep icefall. From a nunatak ("rock island") between the North Mowich and Edmunds glaciers (usual bivouac site), attain the headwall and icefall. Several mid-face rock bands are passed as far left as possible, or climb over the icefall, as some parties have done, to where consistently steep snow and ice leads to the final cliff. Passing the cliff gives access to upper Ptarmigan Ridge.

In recent years, the final rock band has become a very formidable cliff. It is doubtful that an easy or safe route could be found to overcome this obstacle as it presently exists. A direct finish variation has been climbed more recently, which passes the rock band farther right, then skirts below an ice cliff.

This route is technically demanding, and has difficult rock and ice climbing sections. Be prepared to bivouac, and for the possibility of difficult free climbing or direct aid on the final rock band.

Mowich Face routes. (Photo: Austin Post, U.S.Geological Survey)

15 Mowich Face – North Mowich Glacier Headwall ▲

Duration: 12 hrs minimum
Rating: V, Class 5 or aid

This route climbs the left flank of the Mowich Face. From the rock island between the North Mowich and Edmunds glaciers, ascend to the head of the North Mowich Glacier. Continue directly up the headwall, passing several rock bands, and up steep snow and ice slopes to the final cliffs. The original party traversed right around the summit cliffs to the upper shoulder of Liberty Cap. A direct finish has been done, climbing straight up and traversing under the ice cliff to reach the shoulder of Liberty Cap.

This route is technically demanding, and has difficult rock and ice climbing sections with attendant rock and icefall danger. Be prepared to bivouac.

16 Mowich Face – Central ▲

Duration: 8-10 hrs
Rating: IV, Class 4 or 5

This route climbs the central portion of the Mowich Face, and is considered a bit easier than the previous two routes.

From a rock ridge near the head of the Edmunds Glacier, go left across the glacier onto the face. Angle left, passing rock bands mid-face, then continue right beneath several cliffs, passing the upper rock bands via one of several possible routes. In late season, when the direct route is impassible or too dangerous, outflanking the final rock bands has been done, but it can be a very time-consuming alternative.

17 Mowich Face – Edmunds Glacier Headwall ▲ ★

Duration: 8-10 hrs
Rating: III

This was the original route on Mowich Face. From a bivouac on the rock ridge near the head of the Edmunds Glacier, traverse slightly right to the head of the Edmunds Glacier, and ascend the snow and ice slopes directly to join Sunset Ridge. Continue to Liberty Cap. Mostly protected from rockfall, but can have significant avalanche danger.

18 Mowich Face – Sunset Ridge ▲

Duration: 12 hrs
Rating: II, Class 4

A "direct" and unimportant variation of the Sunset Ridge route, which ascends the rightmost margin of the Edmunds Glacier headwall, meeting Sunset Ridge just below the point where the route reaches the ridge crest. This route is a bit more complex than the standard Sunset Ridge route, with additional rockfall hazard, and thus is not recommended.

19 Sunset Ridge ■

Duration: 12 hrs minimum
Rating: III, Class 3 or 4

This prominent ridge flanks Mowich Face on the right. From the head of Colonnade Ridge, traverse the South Mowich Glacier to the cleaver separating South Mowich and Edmunds glaciers. The primary route ascends left of the actual ridge crest via prominent snow and ice slopes and snow gullies (rockfall hazard) to the ridge crest proper. There is a good rest stop atop a rotten rock formation that juts west from the ridge at about 11,800 feet. Continue on a rotten traverse along the crest, or via snow and ice slopes below the crest (better when snow conditions are good), to the easier upper slopes.

This route is long, and will take most parties a full day from high camp. Descents usually are made via the Tahoma Glacier or Sickle. Rockfall is a hazard on this route. Ice screws, a few pitons, and helmets recommended.

20 Sunset Amphitheater ▲

Duration: 10-12 hrs
Rating: III, Class 4 or 5

The Sunset Amphitheater is the large cirque at the head of the South Mowich Glacier. Its headwall is a colorful cliff of alternating bands of andesite, pumice and ash which can appear impassable from a distance, but somewhat more feasible from Sunset Ridge.

Approach via Puyallup Cleaver (as for the Tahoma Glacier route), but continue over and/or around St. Andrews Rocks (very loose) to the headwall. The South Mowich Glacier icefall sometimes is ascended instead of crossing the rocks.

The original route ascends via the shortest possible line to reach the ice cap. It involves some ice climbing to get past the ice cliff, with ice screws recommended. The secondary line essentially begins where the original route does, depending upon bergschrund conditions. Ascend ice slopes and intermittent rock sections to a ramp that leads left across the amphitheater walls to a final exit gully. This route is much more difficult than the original route. Bring ice screws and rock pitons for both routes.

Sunset Amphitheater routes have significant rockfall danger and exposure to avalanches and icefall. None of these routes is popular or particularly recommended.

Puyallup Cleaver Approach

All routes on the west side of Mount Rainier north of and including the Tahoma Glacier commonly are approached via Puyallup Cleaver. Drive up Westside Road from the park entrance, across Round Pass, and down to St. Andrews Creek. (Note: The Westside Road may be closed due to flooding from South Tahoma Glacier and Tahoma Creek.) Hike in via Klapatche Park Trail (Hike 1) to the Wonderland Trail, then south to St. Andrews Lake, where a climbers' trail leads up Puyallup Cleaver past Tokaloo Spire and Tokaloo Rock (Off-Trail Route 2). Continue up the cleaver past the imposing rock buttress (on the left via the Puyallup Glacier), and regain the cleaver at a saddle near 9,000 feet. This is a customary bivouac site.

Puyallup Cleaver suffers from overuse by climbing and cross-country hiking parties. Smaller parties are recommended to lessen impact. Also, use established campsites, or camp on snow to avoid further damage. The Park Service may further limit the number of overnight parties here, and also will be eliminating unauthorized campsites. Off-site camping is a citable offense!

Routes on the Tahoma Glacier and surrounding areas. (Photo: Austin Post, U.S.Geological Survey)

21 Tahoma Glacier ■ ★
Duration: 6-8 hrs one way

One of the six glaciers descending from Mount Rainier's summit plateau, the Tahoma Glacier flows through a narrow gap between Sunset Amphitheater and the Tahoma Cleaver. This is the most popular west-side route, as it is the least technically demanding and most direct route to the summit.

From the bivouac, continue up the Puyallup Glacier left of the cleaver's crest to where the cleaver fades and the slope drops off steeply toward the Tahoma Glacier. Traverse to the central portion of the narrowing glacier and ascend as conditions permit directly to the summit.

Variations to this route exist, but most are not notable or worthy, except that "The Sickle," a usually crevasse-free corridor on the glacier's left side, commonly is used as a descent route in early season. Most parties retrace the route of ascent. The Sickle descent continues directly over crumbly St. Andrews Rocks; most climbers wisely go around the north side when crevasse conditions permit.

Ice cliffs forming on the upper right side of the Tahoma Glacier (where it flows from the summit icecap) pose an increasing threat of icefall here. Helmets are recommended, especially when climbing over or around St. Andrews Rocks.

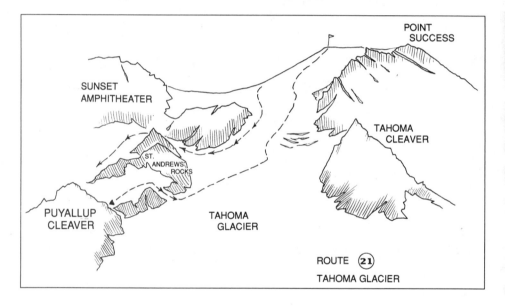

22 Tahoma Cleaver ▲

Duration: 12 hrs minimum
Rating: V, Class 4 or 5

This is the prominent cleaver separating the Tahoma and South Tahoma glaciers. This was the last of Mount Rainier's major ridges to be climbed, and is not a pleasant prospect.

If Tahoma Creek Trail is closed, approach from Mirror Lakes and Success Divide, crossing the South Puyallup Glacier to reach the cleaver. The objective is to reach the crest just above the big gendarme at 11,700 feet, via steep snow slope traverses, and go on to the base of a rock buttress (the "Black Triangle"). From here, there are two possibilities. Either ascend up to a shelf (very loose since a rockfall in 1959) and along the shelf to Point Success, or drop down and ascend snow and ice slopes below a rock band to a crumbly exit via two long, steep, Class 4 pitches on loose rock (the route taken by post-rockfall parties – all one of them).

This route will have considerable rockfall and avalanche hazard and routefinding difficulty. Take ice screws, pitons and a helmet.

Success Divide Approach

Parties climbing South Tahoma Glacier Headwall, Success Cleaver and Success Finger usually approach via Success Divide. Hike to Mirror Lakes via Indian Henry's Hunting Ground (Hikes 5 or 7), then skirt Pyramid Peak (Off-Trail Route 3) on the left side to reach Success Divide. There are comfortable bivouac sites at several places along the divide. Camp on snow whenever possible to minimize your impact.

Success Cleaver and surrounding routes. (Photo: Austin Post, U.S.Geological Survey)

23 South Tahoma Glacier – Headwall ▲

Duration: 10-12 hrs
Rating: III, Class 4 possible

This route climbs the South Tahoma Glacier, through its headwall, to Point Success. The glacier was the site of a 1946 air crash that killed 32 Marines.

Approach as for the Success Cleaver route. Drop onto the glacier and ascend as crevasses permit to the bergschrund deep within the cirque. The headwall reportedly has been climbed by three distinct routes; only one route is shown.

This route has rockfall danger, and is subject to avalanches in early season. Still, early season ascents are suggested for easier climbing and less exposure to rockfall. Without snowcover, it would be a very dangerous climb.

24 Success Cleaver ■

Duration: 10-12 hrs one way
Rating: III, Class 3

Success Cleaver is the long ridge descending from Point Success on the southwest. This is the only route on Mount Rainier that involves no notable glacier travel, but it has loose rock and is a very long climb. Its name is no guarantee of success.

Approach either from Longmire or Tahoma Creek Trail to Indian Henry's Hunting Ground. From there, traverse around the left side of Pyramid Peak onto lower Success Cleaver. Ascend the cleaver on its crest, avoiding most obstacles on the right side, until forced down and right onto the Success Glacier headwall and into a snow gully. Continue up snow or ice slopes between rock bands to where the cleaver merges with the Kautz Cleaver, and continue to Point Success.

Some parties have traversed left across the upper South Tahoma Headwall to the summit plateau, rather than climbing through the rock bands leading to Kautz Cleaver.

In late season, this route involves much loose scrambling. Descending the route is not common, but is a possibility.

25 Success Headwall ■

Duration: 8-10 hrs one way
Rating: III, Class 3 or 4

From Success Divide, descend to the right onto Pyramid Glacier. Continue across the ridge dividing Pyramid and Success Glaciers and contour up the Success Glacier to the headwall. Ascend the rightmost of the three broad couloirs (the "Success Finger") to join Kautz Cleaver. It is possible that the other two couloirs have been ascended (the left couloir was used as a descent route by a 1946 party, although no record of an ascent exists). The leftmost couloir joins the Success Cleaver route. The middle cleaver would appear to involve bypassing or overcoming several rock steps directly through the headwall.

There are no special difficulties on this route as far as Kautz Cleaver. Avalanches and rockfall are a definite possibilities.

Wapowety Cleaver Approach

The Kautz Cleaver and Kautz Headwall routes begin from Wapowety Cleaver, which commonly is approached via Van Trump Park Trail (Hike 10) and the Van Trump Glaciers, although a longer approach may be used along the ridge crest above Mildred Point. Most parties bivouac on the cleaver (several good sites) and cross the Kautz Glacier on the morning of their ascent. Stay on snow as much as possible to minimize your impact.

26 Kautz Cleaver ■
Duration: 12 hrs
Rating: III, Class 3

This is the rock spur separating the Success and Kautz glaciers. Approach from Christine Falls and Van Trump Park, or from Mirror Lakes via Success Glacier. Cross the Kautz Glacier above the icefall at 9,000 feet to the base of Kautz Cleaver, and ascend the cleaver to near Point Success. Several rock bands must be bypassed to gain the summit. Don't rule out a bivouac. Be prepared for rockfall.

27 Kautz Glacier – Headwall ■ ★
Duration: 8-10 hrs
Rating: III, Class 3 or 4

This increasingly popular route climbs the headwall above the lower portion of the Kautz Glacier, immediately right of Kautz Cleaver. Approach as for Kautz Cleaver, but ascend the Wapowety Cleaver to about 10,000 feet instead of crossing the glacier (or, alternatively, descend from Camp Hazard). Traverse onto the glacier and ascend the snow finger up the headwall to where rock bands must be passed or avoided to reach Point Success.

There are no special difficulties on this route when there is sufficient snow to allow climbers to avoid the rock bands. It is steep, with occasional avalanche or rockfall, but is said to be very enjoyable by those who have climbed it.

Camp Hazard Approach

The Kautz Glacier and Wilson Glacier Headwall routes begin from Paradise. Ascend the Skyline Trail to Glacier Vista (Hike 11), and descend to the Nisqually Glacier. Cross the glacier as crevasses allow, and gain a prominent gully dividing cliffs on the other side. Ascend this to the left edge of the Wilson Glacier. Continue up and left along the glacier's edge.

To reach Camp Hazard, ascend snowfields (via several possible routes) toward the ice cliff. The camp is only a flat spot on the ridge well below the ice cliffs. Don't expect a hut or shelter here. The camp is named for early explorer and writer Joseph Hazard, and not because it is in a precarious position.

The other routes (Wilson Glacier Headwall, Fuhrer Thumb and Fuhrer Finger) begin from Wilson Glacier. Approaches over the glacier will be dictated by crevasse conditions.

Stay on snow and ice as much as possible to minimize your impact here. Also, use blue bags for waste disposal, please!

28 Kautz Glacier – Ice Cliff ● ★
Duration: 4-6 hrs

This route follows the approximate line attempted by Kautz in 1857. Kautz and party are credited with getting near 13,000 feet in elevation. The route was used by guided parties after the collapse of Gibraltar Ledge in 1936.

From Camp Hazard, descend slightly onto the Kautz Glacier, skirt the ice cliff area and climb a steep ice chute to reach the upper glacier. Continue up moderate glacier slopes to the summit. Bring some ice screws for the chute. A long crevasse that requires skirting recently has formed at about 12,000 feet.

Kautz Glacier routes. (Photo: Austin Post, U.S.Geological Survey)

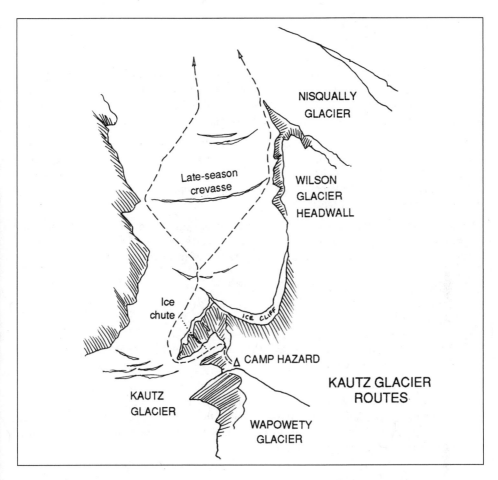

KAUTZ GLACIER ROUTES

29 Wilson Glacier – Headwall ▲

Duration: 6-8 hrs
Rating: II, Class 4 or 5

This route climbs ice chutes through the headwall above Wilson Glacier and, like Fuhrer Finger, is a direct route to the summit in early season.

Approach from Paradise as for the Kautz Glacier route. Ascend a snow finger and ice chutes (two possibilities) on the left side of the headwall, left of a prominent rock buttress. Continue to the crest and across the summit plateau to the crater rim.

Beware of icefall from the Kautz ice cliffs, and of avalanches. In late season, a rock step has to be negotiated. Rockfall is a hazard during normal conditions. Descent via Fuhrer Finger is most common.

A variation ("Fuhrer Thumb") ascends the prominent couloir between the Wilson Glacier headwall and Fuhrer Finger. It is steeper and narrower than Fuhrer Finger, and has higher rockfall hazard. The couloir is split at the bottom by rock outcroppings, permitting variations at the beginning and end that eventually connect with the Fuhrer Finger route. A bergschrund may present a problem later in the year.

30 Fuhrer Finger ● ★
Duration: 3-5 hrs

This is considered the fastest route to the summit of Mount Rainier, and sometimes is climbed in one day round trip from Paradise. It first was climbed by guides Hans and Heinie Fuhrer, with Joseph Hazard and others, in 1920. In August 1934, park ranger Bill Butler made a round trip from Paradise to the summit in 11 hrs, 20 minutes!

Approach as for Kautz Glacier, or cross the Nisqually Glacier directly to the base of the gully (a less avalanche-prone approach for early season). Continue into the obvious snow finger on the right side of the upper Wilson Glacier, and up to the upper Nisqually Glacier. From the top of the chute, ascend along the upper left margin of the Nisqually Glacier, or more directly if feasible.

Beware of killer avalanches down the chute. Glissading down the chute is not at all recommended for safety reasons. Rockfall is likely in later season and on warm afternoons. The chute becomes unsafe in late August of most years.

31 Nisqually Icefall ▲ ★
Duration: 6-8 hrs
Rating: III

This route ascends the steep and heavily-fractured Nisqually Glacier as it is squeezed down from the summit ice plateau.

Traverse from Camp Muir to the center of the Nisqually Glacier and ascend the icefall as is practical, depending upon serac conditions. This route has significant icefall and rockfall danger, particularly while passing below the ice cliff, the icefall and Gibraltar Chute. Nevertheless, it is increasingly popular, no doubt because of its menacing nature, technical difficulty and easy accessibility.

32 Nisqually Ice Cliff ▲
Duration: 6-8 hrs
Rating: III, Class 4 or 5

This route ascends the eastern lobe of the upper Nisqually Glacier, passing beneath an immense ice cliff. It was ascended in 1962 by Barry Bishop and Lute Jerstad, who together climbed Mount Everest as members of the 1963 American Mount Everest Expedition.

Descend from Camp Muir around Cowlitz Cleaver, then up the Nisqually Glacier to the ice cliff. Ascend an ice chute on the extreme left side of the ice cliff (and not the ice cliff proper) onto the upper glacier.

A variation ascends left from the top of the ice chute onto the Nisqually Cleaver, where loose Class 4 rock leads to the upper glacier. Another variation has climbed the Nisqually Cleaver directly from its base; this has horribly loose Class 5 rock climbing, and is not recommended. Yet another variation climbs the chute below the ice cliff up to Gibraltar Ledge. This has high rockfall danger, as well as icefall hazard from the ice cliff, and is not the least bit recommended. Bring ice screws, a few pitons, and a helmet for all variations.

Nisqually Ice Fall. (Photo: Austin Post, U.S.Geological Survey)

Little Tahoma Peak

Little Tahoma Peak is a craggy remnant of the once-higher volcano. It is largely unstable, and is being undercut by glaciers on both sides, particularly by the Emmons Glacier. In 1963, a massive rockfall occurred on the peak's north face, scattering debris on the glacier below and obliterating the only route climbed on that face so far. Although a mere satellite peak of Mount Rainier, Little Tahoma, at 11,138 ft/3395 m, stands taller than most summits in the Cascade Range. It is a popular ascent, mostly because of its elevation, offering challenge for climbers of all abilities. Little Tahoma is a technical climb, and is not recommended for inexperienced climbers or scramblers because it requires glacier travel and has very loose rock. It is a popular winter and spring ski ascent, via the standard route and Fryingpan Glacier, but skiers don't go to the summit, which can be a very dangerous objective during winter. A climbing card is required for ascents of Little Tahoma Peak.

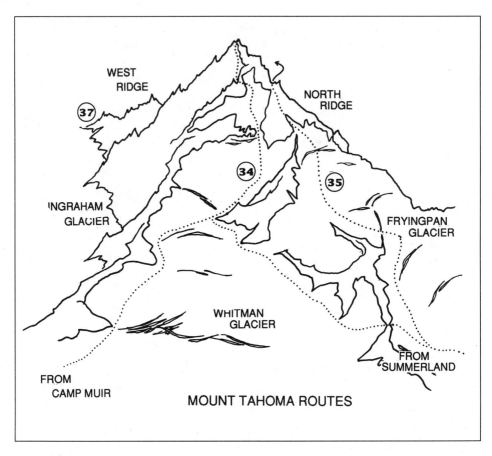

WEST RIDGE

NORTH RIDGE

37

34

35

INGRAHAM GLACIER

FRYINGPAN GLACIER

WHITMAN GLACIER

FROM SUMMERLAND

FROM CAMP MUIR

MOUNT TAHOMA ROUTES

33 Whitman Glacier (East Shoulder) ● ★
Duration: 4-6 hrs
Rating: Class 3

This was the route used by J.B. Flett and H.H. Garrison in 1895 during the first ascent of Little Tahoma.

The route may be approached two ways. Most parties approach from Summerland via the Wonderland Trail (Hike 25), continuing to Meany Crest and crossing the Fryingpan Glacier to a notch in Whitman Crest. From the notch, the route descends onto the Whitman Glacier and joins the other approach. This comes from Paradise via the Skyline Trail (as for Camp Muir), but breaks off across the Cowlitz Glacier below Anvil Rock. The second approach continues across the Ingraham Glacier and reaches the Whitman Glacier via a broad gap in the east ridge of Little Tahoma. Because of time, complexity and greater crevasse danger, the Summerland approach is recommended, unless you already are camped at Camp Muir. The final pinnacle is a very short but loose scrambling ascent.

34 Northeast Face ▲
Duration: 8-10 hrs
Rating: III, Class 4 or 5

The northeast face of Little Tahoma rises above the head of the Fryingpan Glacier. It is a technical and demanding ascent and is not popular.

Approach from Summerland onto the Fryingpan Glacier, as for the standard route. Go right of the notch, passing beneath a large buttress, to the head of the glacier. The route climbs the face above, trending towards the skyline, and eventually traversing right around the summit formation. The major cliff band at 9,500 feet was passed on the east side by the first ascent party, which reported that the route up to the ridge was dictated by the conditions encountered, including snow and ice passages through the rotten rock, with steep ice frequently requiring placement of ice pitons. The summit pinnacle was reached by passing the right skyline pinnacle on the north and ascending a difficult steep rock pitch just east of the pinnacle. Traverse about 100 meters across loose "shingle" rock to a notch, where three consecutive rock pillars are climbed directly to the summit.

This route has rockfall danger. Helmets, pitons and ice screws/pitons are recommended.

35 North Face ◆
Duration: 6-8 hrs
Rating: III, Class 5?

The north face of Little Tahoma was climbed in 1959, but never repeated. In 1963, a massive rockfall destroyed much of the route and left the face highly unstable. No attempts have been reported since the first ascent. Even then, it was considered a suicide route. Those wishing to push their luck should first refer to *The Challenge of Rainier.*

36 West Ridge ◆
Duration: 12 hrs minimum
Rating: V, Class 5

The spiny west ridge of Little Tahoma was considered the last major unclimbed route on Mount Rainier. Early attempts were thwarted by unstable, difficult rock. The first ascent was made during winter conditions to avoid loose rock.

The route may be approached most easily via Cathedral Gap from Camp Muir. The first ascent party bypassed loose rock via difficult ice climbing, with 18 belayed pitches and three rappels from gendarmes. Unless well-frozen, this route is unsafe; even when frozen, it is more difficult than Curtis Ridge. Like the Northeast Face route, the route taken largely will be dictated by prevailing conditions. Ice screws, rock pitons and helmets recommended.

These climbers explore the firn caves at the summit of Mount Rainier. (Photo: National Park Service)

Chapter Eight:
Winter Recreation

Along with its many summertime activities, Mount Rainier National Park is a favorite destination of winter recreation enthusiasts. There are dozens of cross-country ski routes, ranging from easy one-day road tours to multi-day wildnerness tours, plus many technical ski mountaineering routes on and around Mount Rainier. Almost any summer hiking destination can be reached on skis or snowshoes. There is a groomed inner-tube run at Paradise, as well as several ski tours and snowshoe hikes originating from this winter-recreation hub. Snowmobiles are permitted within the park, but on a very restricted basis; they are permitted on Stevens Canyon Road, Westside Road and White River Road, to certain points, and could be used by skiers and snowshoers to shorten access time to several places. If you're lucky, you might hitch a ride!

Winter backcountry travel is a way to lessen potential impact on wilderness areas of Mount Rainier National Park. Snow cover helps protect fragile plant communities and eliminates human-caused erosion.

Snow camping is a popular winter activity. Overnight visitors should be mindful that park regulations limit both the size of your party and where you can set up camp. During winter months, when snow cover is greater than 2 feet (5 feet at Paradise), you may camp anywhere you wish, so long as you are more than 200 feet from plowed roads and parking areas (so you don't get buried by snowblowers!), 100 feet from lakes and streams, and 300 feet from buildings. Party size is limited to 12 persons, except near Paradise; larger groups at Paradise must be between 300 feet and 600 feet of restrooms and must use them! Also, backcountry permits are required for snow camping. You are not permitted to sleep in your car except at Sunshine Point Campground, the park's only year-round campground – and then only if you register. In winter, backcountry permits may be obtained from the Nisqually Entrance, Longmire Museum, Paradise Visitor Center, Ohanapecosh ranger station, and the U.S. Forest Service White River Ranger District office in Enumclaw. Call the Backcountry Desk at (206) 569-2211 or White River Ranger District office at (206) 825-6585 for information on winter permit availability.

Again, almost any destination in the park can be reached on skis or snowshoes. Indeed, the summit of Mount Rainier has been reached on skis, and Liberty Ridge has been descended by a brave (or is it foolish?) skier. The routes described here are some of the more popular and scenic winter tours. When you have done all of these, and if you are still feeling ambitious, try something different.

Ski Mountaineering

This guide will not discuss specific ski mountaineering routes on Mount Rainier, except to say that skiers have descended the Ingraham Glacier, Nisqually Glacier, Tahoma Glacier, Furher Finger and Emmons Glacier, to name several, and even routes as steep as Liberty Ridge. Snowboarders have descended from Mount Rainier's summit by various routes, and

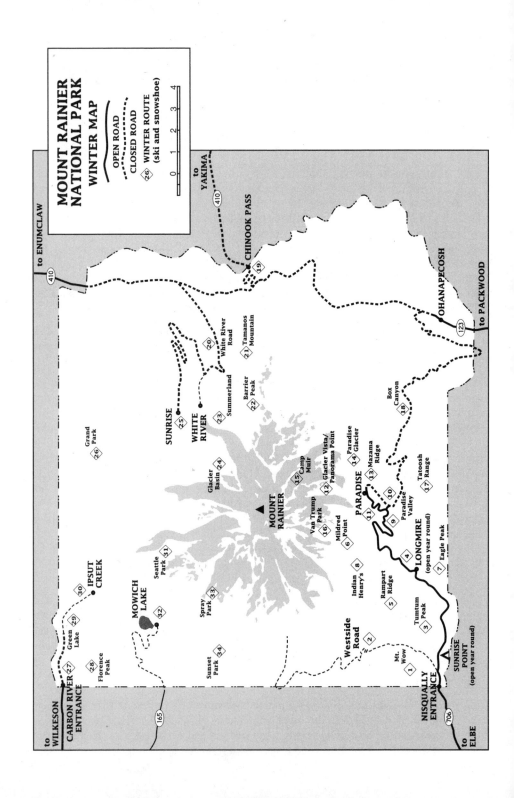

MOUNT RAINIER
NATIONAL PARK
WINTER MAP

OPEN ROAD
CLOSED ROAD
26 WINTER ROUTE
(ski and snowshoe)

0 1 2 3 4

no doubt will continue to do so as the sport increases in popularity. Obviously, if Liberty Ridge can be descended on skis, there are only a few routes on Mount Rainier that definitely cannot be skied. However, the risks are very great. This guide's purpose is to aid you in your enjoyment and exploration of Mount Rainier National Park, not to recommend death-defying acts and foolish stunts. If you insist upon making extreme ski descents of Mount Rainier, go for it, but at your peril. Ski mountaineering should not be attempted by inexperienced skiers or anyone without mountaineering skills and experience.

Use the following symbols to tell whether each route is suitable for skiing or snowshoeing:

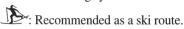 : Recommended as a ski route.

🏃 : Recommended as a snowshoe hike.

The following symbols will denote the level of difficulty of these ski and snowshoe trips, so you have a better idea of which tours are appropriate for you.

● - Appropriate for all abilities: No special difficulties; low to moderate exposure to avalanche danger. If you ski slow and straight ahead, you can handle it!

■ - Intermediate: Steeper terrain and routefinding difficulties may be encountered, along with increased exposure to avalanche danger. If you can't climb or turn on downhill runs, you shouldn't be here.

▲ - Advanced: Difficult snow conditions and routefinding; subject to higher avalanche risk. Not for the inexperienced or unprepared. If you can ski very well downhill, and are skilled at staying safe and alive, you may proceed.

◆ - Expert: Mountaineering experience and equipment recommended. Very difficult skiing with tremendous exposure to avalanches, weather and other risks.

Routes marked with ⑫ are hiking trails; those marked with ⑿ are off-trail routes.

You will have to decide for yourself what equipment to bring for a given ski route. Hints are given as to type of skiing terrain to be encountered, but each skier will have a preference of the type of skis to bring. Just don't bring touring skis for telemarking or ski mountaineering!

Stay off plowed roads and other roads open to auto traffic! Visibility is poor, cars can't stop very fast on snow and ice, and neither can you. If you attempt to ski or even walk down a snowy or icy road, you are asking for trouble.

Winter Auto Travel

Auto travel within the park during winter can be treacherous. Paradise Highway is the only road open all winter, but it can be closed by heavy snowfall and avalanches. The road is gated at Longmire each evening at about 5 p.m. and does not reopen until the next morning, or as soon as road conditions permit safe travel. Check with rangers or signs at Longmire for times of gate closure and opening. Plan to leave early enough to avoid being locked in! Also, when waiting for the gate to open, don't line up on the roadway. Stay in the parking lot, parked head-in to the snowbanks. Never park on the roadway during winter. Tire chains must be carried in all vehicles traveling within the park during winter. All-wheel drive vehicles with approved snow tires sometimes are exempt from the "chains required" advisory, but if conditions are bad, you must still have a set of chains. Be aware that, even though you can safely make the climb to Paradise without chains, your return to

Longmire will require frequent braking and icy turns. Reduce your speed, use low gears, and use brakes sparingly. Make sure to leave extra space between your car and other vehicles to compensate for longer stopping distances. If you start skidding, don't slam on the brakes! Instead, ease off the gas pedal and turn in the direction of your skid until you regain traction (this is the Park Service's recommendation, so if it doesn't work, don't blame me). Also, watch out for snowplows and snowblowers. Make sure snowplowing operations are completed before you drive downhill in the morning. Turn on your headlights for extra visibility at all times, and don't drive too close to the centerline. You should phone ahead to make sure of road conditions before planning a winter visit to Mount Rainier.

Also, remember not to set your emergency brake if possible, as they frequently freeze solid overnight.

Safety Rules for Winter Travel

The major considerations for winter recreation within the park are weather and snow conditions. Mount Rainier's weather is unpredictable enough during the summer season; during the winter, fierce storms lasting several days at a time are not uncommon. Snowfall and high winds accompany these storms, and whiteout conditions are frequent, particularly above timberline. Parties have become lost and pinned down for days by storms, and fatalities have occured. Indeed, as this guide neared its completion, yet another skier vanished above Paradise.

Although foul weather is the major hazard for winter backcountry travelers, avalanches are more feared. Avalanches can range from minor snow sluffs to huge slabs capable of burying everything in their path. The high volume of snowfall, wind-accumulated snow, and rapidly changing weather patterns account for particularly high avalanche danger in

Park naturalist Ron Warfield leads a snowshoe hike at Paradise. (Photo: Loren Lane)

Here are a few basic rules for winter travel within Mount Rainier National Park:

• NEVER TRAVEL ALONE!

• Check weather and avalanche conditions prior to every trip. Don't go out during poor weather or high avalanche danger if you can avoid it. Avalanche Hotlines: (206) 526-6677, or (503) 326-2400.

• Let someone know where you are going before your trip (there is no day registration).

• Never travel during or immediately after a snowstorm. The time needed to allow snow to stabilize is an often-debated question – it is up to you and your better judgment.

• Carry avalanche cords (or better, avalanche beacons), probe poles and a collapsible snow shovel whenever on or below potential avalanche slopes.

• Avoid soft, steep snow slopes and leeward slopes.

• Learn about avalanches and how to avoid them. Also learn avalanche search and rescue techniques before your trip. Always be prepared for a search and rescue. This means every member of your party should carry probe poles, a snow shovel and an avalanche transceiver.

• When crossing a suspect slope, expect to be buried, and prepare accordingly. Button up, put on mittens and a hat, loosen your pack and ski pole straps, and turn your avalanche beacon to "transmit" mode (or tie on an avalanche cord). Only one person at a time should cross to safer ground ("The family that tours close together is buried close together"), and everyone else should watch carefully. Stay high if possible.

• Potential avalanche paths should be used only if there is no other feasible route, and then only with extreme caution.

• When traveling above treeline in questionable weather, wand your route so you can find your way back if a storm sets in.

• Travel on ridge lines instead of open slopes.

• On overnight trips, take enough food and fuel to last two extra days, and take a snow shovel on extended hikes and tours so you can dig in (or out) if things get really bad.

• If caught in a whiteout, stop! If you keep descending in a whiteout, you may ski over a cliff. If you can't stop, at least slow down and be careful where you step.

• Bring a whistle. The sound of a whistle carries much farther than a voice during a storm or whiteout. Rescuers may not be able to see you if you are lost or injured, but if they can hear you, they will be better able to find you.

some areas, under certain conditions. The park service will provide, upon request, several handouts on winter travel and avalanche safety. Ask for them and read them carefully before you embark on your winter journey.

Warm, wet weather or a rapidly rising temperature with accompanying wind are common warning signs of avalanche danger, and during such weather, particularly after a snowfall, open snow slopes should be avoided. During unstable snow conditions, almost anything can trigger an avalanche. Beware of shifts in wind direction, freezing rain and rising temperatures, and stay off unstable slopes. Skiers should be familiar with recognizing and avoiding dangerous avalanche slopes, as well as avalanche rescue techniques, before they venture into snow country.

Avoiding potential avalanche slopes is the best way to avoid getting caught in an avalanche. Stay off steep, open slopes, and out of steep gullies.

Avalanche Survival and Rescue

If you are caught in an avalanche, do everything you can to stay on top of the sliding snow. Discard all equipment and try swimming atop the avalanche. This may keep you on the surface. If you can't stay on top, and are buried, close your mouth and eyes and cover your face with your arms. This will help create an airspace. As the snow stops sliding, try to enlarge your airspace before the snow solidifies, which is usually instantaneous. If you have time, dig furiously towards the surface if you can tell which way to dig (remember that spit falls down, so spit, watch where it falls, then dig in the opposite direction). If you are lucky, you will get an arm out and create an air hole, which may permit you to be found and rescued more quickly. If you can't get out, try to relax and wait. Conserve your air by staying calm and breathing slowly. Chances of survival are reduced by more than half after half an hour of burial, so the more you can do to conserve your precious air, the better your chances of survival. Because of avalanche danger alone, it is very unwise to travel alone in winter. Parties of three are a recommended minimum.

If a companion is buried in an avalanche, don't panic! Watch and make a note of the last place you saw the victim. After making sure all surviving members are safe, make a visual

An ice avalanche cascades down Mount Rainier's steep Willis Wall. (Photo: Ashael Curtis, courtesy National Park Service)

search of the entire avalanche area for clues. This is where avalanche transceivers come in handy. Mark areas where you last saw the victim, and begin your search. If you can't locate anything, start probing in accumulation areas first, using an avalanche probe, ski pole or ice axe (in that order), as avalanche victims are buried 4½ feet deep, on average. Be careful, but be fast! Don't stop looking until help arrives. If you are the only person around, you are the victim's only chance for survival. Unless reliable help is less than 15 minutes away, you must do your best to find the victim immediately.

Reading *The ABC of Avalanche Safety* and taking an avalanche safety course is a good idea before you venture into the backcountry during winter.

Avalanche Danger Warnings

There are four levels of avalanche danger, one of which is posted daily at the Nisqually Entrance:

Low Hazard: Mostly stable snow conditions exist and avalanches are unlikely (but still possible), except in isolated pockets on steep snow-covered open slopes and gullies. Backcountry travel generally is safe in areas with low hazard.

Moderate Hazard: Areas of unstable snow exist and avalanches are possible on steep snow-covered open slopes and gullies. Backcountry travelers should use caution in areas with moderate hazard.

High Hazard: Mostly unstable snow conditions exist and avalanches are likely on steep snow-covered open slopes and gullies. Backcountry travel is not recommended except in avalanche-free areas.

Extreme Hazard: Widespread areas of unstable snow exist and avalanches are certain on steep snow-covered open slopes and gullies. Backcountry travel is not recommended except in avalanche-free areas. Backcountry travel should be avoided. (Auto travel also should be avoided, if possible.)

Hypothermia is another very real danger to winter travelers in Mount Rainier National Park, perhaps more threatening than avalanches. Freezing temperatures, wet snow and wind all conspire against us, especially at higher elevations where exposure to wind is greater. All winter backcountry travelers must do everything possible to stay warm and dry, and sheltered from the wind. Wearing wool or synthetic garments can keep you insulated even when you get wet, but rain and windproof outer garments are a must in terms of staying dry. Snacking frequently will keep your metabolism rate higher, thus keeping you warmer. Also, if you get cold and wet, get out of the wind and weather and dry off as soon as possible. The longer you are exposed to poor winter weather, the greater your chances of becoming hypothermic. Preventing hypothermia is much easier than treating it later.

Just as this guide cannot provide mountaineering instruction, it also cannot provide a thorough lesson on avalanche safety, snow travel, orienteering, or winter survival strategies. Winter visitors should learn about avalanches, including prediction and rescue, before they find themselves or a companion buried, and should know how to prepare for winter travel before they find themselves lost in a blizzard. Obviously, skiers should know how to ski so they don't hurt themselves or others. Snowshoes are not the easiest things to use, either, so it might help to practice putting them on and walking around before you head off into the winter wonderland. And everyone should know how to avoid and treat frostbite and hypothermia.

An oft-neglected hazard of winter backcountry travel is snow falling from trees. After heavy snowfalls and during warming periods, snow accumulations on trees regularly slough off. These snow bombs can cause serious injury and sometimes even death, so watch out below!

There are a few opportunities within Mount Rainier National Park for technical ice climbing up frozen waterfalls. A drive to Paradise on a cold winter day will reveal a half-dozen frozen waterfalls "in shape" for an ascent. Because no accurate records exist concerning such climbs, none will be mentioned in this guide. Any technical ice routes may be reported to the author, care of the publisher, for inclusion in future editions of this guide.

Many "snowshoe hikes" may be done without snowshoes, particularly in spring, provided you don't mind plunging in up to your waist every so often. Be prepared to get wet and cold no matter what your mode of winter travel.

Round-trip time estimates are provided for the reader's convenience, although they are very rough estimates based on the assumption that most parties average about one mile per hour on snow (except for downhill skiing, which obviously is faster). As with all other time estimates in this guide, they are not absolute. Your actual time may vary, but don't plan to take less time for any of these trips. Multi-day trips with basecamps are popular. How long you stay and how far you go is up to you and the weather.

Ski and snowshoe rentals and lessons are available at Longmire. Contact Mount Rainier Guest Services at (206) 569-2275 for details.

● ❄❄❄ ●

1 Mount Wow 🚶 ▲
Duration: 8 hrs

Mount Wow sits at the park's southwest corner, and offers breathtaking views of Mount Rainier. You can hike more or less straight up the west boundary line to the crest of Mount Wow's southwest ridge, which leads upward to the summit crest. Alternatively, from Westside Road, climb more or less directly to Lake Allen and to the ridge crest. Don't climb the Dry Creek avalanche slope!

The summit crest often is firm enough to dispose of snowshoes, so crampons and an ice axe should be available for safe travel as conditions warrant.

2 Westside Road 🎿 ●
Duration: 2-8 hrs

Westside Road road offers easy touring all the way to Round Pass (7 mi), with the opportunity for short side tours along Tahoma Creek. It is possible to continue all the way to North Puyallup River, at the end of the road, although there is increasing avalanche danger as you venture beyond Round Pass. Snowmobiles are permitted on Westside Road, but only as far as Round Pass or the Dry Creek avalanche track, depending upon snow and road conditions. Beware of the avalanche track at Dry Creek, and stay off the beaver ponds!

3 Tumtum Peak

Duration: 4-6 hrs

Tumtum Peak (4,678 ft/1426 m) is the low, heavily-wooded peak just west of Kautz Creek and north of Paradise Highway. It is reached easily on snowshoes by hiking 1 mi to the bridge crossing of Kautz Creek, then up to the ridge crest just north of the peak (via Kautz Creek Trail, Hike 5). The summit is a reasonable, woodsy snow hike south from the bridge.

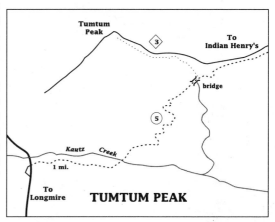

The hike up to Mount Ararat is longer and has a bit more avalanche exposure. Follow the approximate line of Kautz Creek Trail. From the saddle below Mount Ararat, Indian Henry's Hunting Ground is reached easily; beware the descent, which is very avalanche-prone.

4 Longmire

Longmire is a popular cross-country ski hub, especially because equipment may be rented at the National Park Inn.

Snowshoers can wander off in almost any direction from Longmire, so long as they are mindful to avoid ski trails and avalanche paths.

Trail of the Shadows: Trail of the Shadows nature trail is an easy ski or snowshoe hike, offering mostly level snow. Skiing in Longmire Meadows is popular, but stay off the beaver ponds.

Longmire Campground: Longmire Campground is accessible in winter, providing easy terrain for beginning skiers.

Cougar Rock Campground: Located just up Paradise Highway from Longmire, Cougar Rock Campground offers flat, easy skiing for beginners. However, Cougar Rock Campground also is open for snowmobile use, discouraging most ski use.

5 Rampart Ridge

Duration: 4 hrs

Lower Rampart Ridge (Hike 6) is easily accessible, offering good views on clear days. Follow the approximate route of the trail to the ridge crest, then stay near the ridge crest to the Wonderland Trail junction (if you can find it). Loop back via the Wonderland Trail and finish in Longmire Meadows.

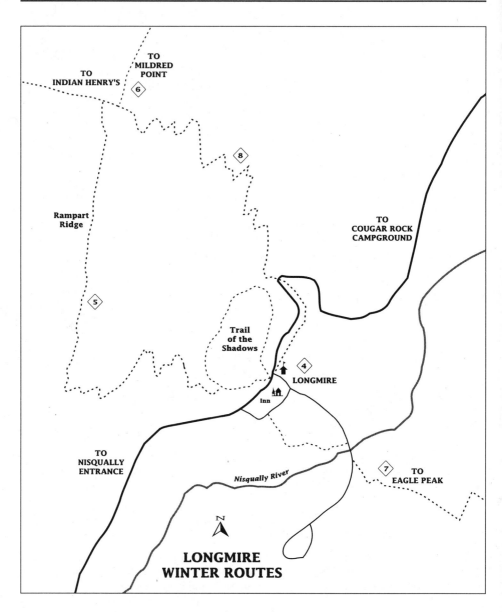

6 Mildred Point 🏂 ▲
Duration: 6-8 hrs

The snowshoe trip to Mildred Point is long (about 8 mi round trip), which discourages most from making this trip. However, on a clear day, the views are tremendous, and there is rarely any avalanche danger on this route. Hike the approximate route of the Wonderland Trail to Rampart Ridge Trail junction (Hike 7), then follow the ridge upward through trees to the open slopes below Mildred Point.

7 Eagle Peak Saddle 🎿 ■
Duration: 6-8 hrs

Although the Eagle Peak Trail (Hike 8) passes through some open areas, the snowshoe route stays pretty much in the trees and is fairly sheltered from avalanche paths. Pick your route carefully to avoid avalanche danger, following the approximate route of the trail. From the saddle, Chutla Peak (6,000 ft/1829+ m) is the winter objective, although usually there is high avalanche danger on its slopes. It is easy to get off-route here, so if you end up below Chutla-Wahpenayo saddle, go back; there is very high avalanche danger below these peaks.

8 Indian Henry's Hunting Ground 🎿 🎿 ▲
Duration: 8-12 hrs

The winter route to Indian Henry's follows the Wonderland Trail from Longmire (Hike 7). The route is equally enjoyable on skis or snowshoes, although either way, an overnight trip with basecamp touring is recommended. There is little avalanche danger on this trip, assuming you stay near the trail. This is not recommended for beginners, as it is a very long tour with some routefinding challenge.

Possible alternative routes are Kautz Creek Trail (Hike 5) or Rampart Ridge directly from Longmire (Hike 6).

9 Paradise Valley 🎿 🎿 ▲
Duration: 2-6 hrs

The Narada Falls parking area is plowed during winter, with a comfort station and trail register, and with straightforward but strenuous access to Paradise via a marked ski trail. The trail climbs gradually beside Paradise River, meeting Stevens Canyon road to cross the river, then along the other side of the river before turning off to the Paradise parking lot. Going downhill is much less work, and many prefer to begin from Paradise for this reason. Snowshoers usually begin from Narada Falls and ascend to Paradise, and are cautioned to stay off the marked ski trail to avoid collisions.

A more difficult ski tour is to descend from Narada Falls to Longmire. This requires very good routefinding skills, but is challenging and enjoyable, or so say those who have made the descent. An all-day ski descent goes from Camp Muir to Paradise, then down Paradise River to Longmire. More reasonable for most parties is to ski to Longmire from Paradise, and have a ride waiting.

10 Reflection Lakes 🎿 🎿 ● or ■
Duration: 4 hrs

Reflection Lakes are accessible by two common routes. Skiers and snowshoers commonly begin from Narada Falls. Skiers also can begin from Paradise. Follow either the Stevens Canyon Road (skis and snowshoes, some avalanche danger) or the marked trail from Paradise Valley Road over Mazama Ridge (skiers only, steeper but less avalanche prone) to the lakes. Stay off the lakes!

Adverse winter use near Reflection Lakes is causing the Park Service some concern. Camp no closer than 100 feet from lakes and streams, and pack out your garbage.

11 Paradise 🎿 🏂 ●, ■ and ▲

Paradise is the winter recreation hub of Mount Rainier National Park. There are plenty of ski and snowshoe trails here for all abilities. The following is not a complete list. Sign in at the visitor center or ranger station trail register. Snowshoers can wander off in any direction, but are advised to avoid marked ski trails, and to stay close to trees whenever possible, so they don't get flattened by enthusiastic skiers or avalanches.

Barn Flats: A flat area just south of the visitor center that is preferred by beginners.

Nisqually Vista: This is a marked route following the Nisqually Vista nature trail from the visitor center. Although this trail would be easy for snowshoers to follow, it is better to leave this to the skiers. Not a good choice for beginners, with its many ups and downs and turns.

Edith Creek Basin: Another unmarked trail, this one leads from Paradise Inn to Edith Creek Basin, which is below and east of Alta Vista. Watch out for avalanches from Alta Vista's highly-prone slopes! It is possible for experienced skiers to join the Glacier Vista route for the descent, or vice versa.

Paradise Valley Road: This unplowed road can be skied from Paradise to the Narada Falls ski trail. Avalanche danger can be very high, though, so it is recommended this route be skied only during periods of stable snow.

Ranger-led Snowshoe Walks: During the week following Christmas, and on weekends through March (or earlier if the snowpack is too thin to protect plant life in Paradise Meadows), park naturalists lead snowshoe hikes from the visitor center. Hike times are 10:30 a.m. and 2:30 p.m. These hikes are open to the first 25 persons to sign up, on a first-come, first-served basis. The sign-up sheet is located at the Jackson Visitor Center, and sign ups begin one hour before each walk. Sign up early! No previous experience is necessary, so if you can walk, you can join the tour. If you don't have snowshoes, you can "rent" a pair for a $1 donation.

Paradise Snowplay Area

A snowplay area consisting of two groomed innertube runs is provided at Paradise. Sliding is permitted only on soft devices and innertubes. No hard sleds, such as toboggans or runner sleds, are permitted. If in doubt, call ahead to see if your sledding device is prohibited. When the snowpack reaches 5 feet in depth, the snowplay area is opened. The runs are groomed and supervised on weekends only; during the week, the runs are not groomed or supervised, but you still can use them if you wish. The park service considers snow sliding to be among the most dangerous winter activities within the park. Be careful! Make sure the run is clear before you launch into your slide. Collisions often cause injury, so do your best to avoid them. Also, dress warmly and expect to get cold and wet. A compressed air station is provided for inflating innertubes.

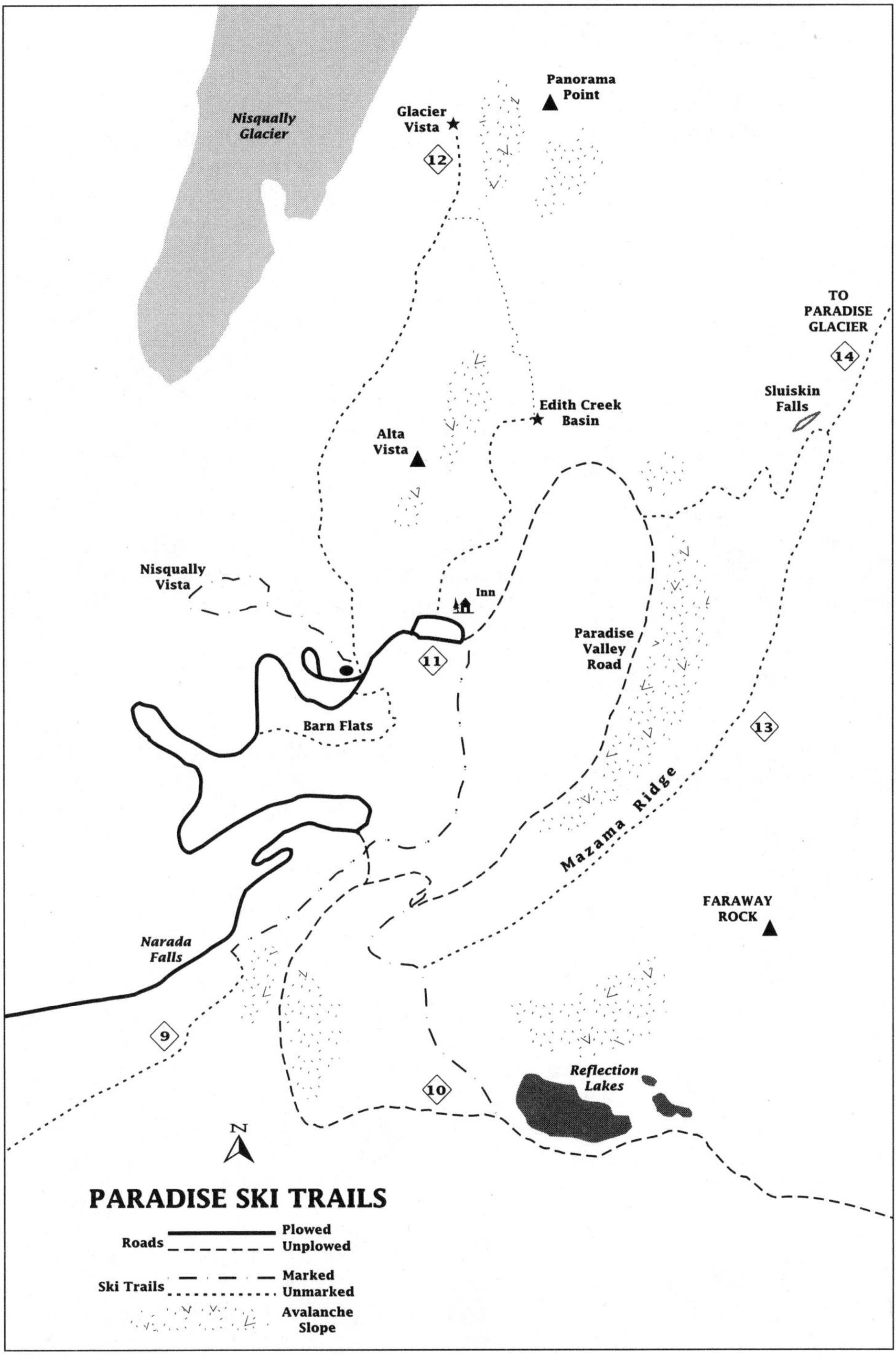

Nisqually Glacier

Glacier Vista ★

◇12◇

Panorama Point ▲

TO PARADISE GLACIER

◇14◇

Sluiskin Falls

Edith Creek Basin ★

Alta Vista ▲

Nisqually Vista

Inn

Paradise Valley Road

Barn Flats

Mazama Ridge

◇13◇

FARAWAY ROCK ▲

◇11◇

Narada Falls

◇9◇

◇10◇

Reflection Lakes

N

PARADISE SKI TRAILS

Roads	—————— Plowed
	– – – – Unplowed
Ski Trails	–·–·– Marked
	·········· Unmarked
░░░	Avalanche Slope

12 Glacier Vista/Panorama Point 🎿 🚶 ■
Duration: 3-6 hrs

This unmarked trail begins from the Paradise visitor center and climbs the approximate route of Deadhorse Creek Trail to Glacier Vista, below the slopes of Panorama Point. The views are spectacular. The slopes leading to Panorama Point and those above are very avalanche-prone, so you are advised to stop at this point. Those venturing higher are advised to stay near the trees on the ridge rather than risk the open slopes.

13 Mazama Ridge 🎿 🚶 ▲
Duration: 6 hrs

Follow the Paradise Valley Road east from the parking lot to the bridge crossing Paradise River, and climb the slopes east to Mazama Ridge, being careful to avoid the highly-prone avalanche slopes. There is a safe route between the avalanche paths. Descend the west side of the ridge to where you join the marked trail from Paradise Valley Road. The trail descends through trees to Reflection Lakes, from where you can take the Stevens Canyon road back to the Narada Falls Trail. Avalanche hazards abound, especially on the slopes of Mazama Ridge above Paradise Valley Road, so take care.

14 Paradise Glacier 🎿 ▲
Duration: 8 hrs

Begin as for Mazama Ridge, but head up the ridge toward the glacier. There are many avalanche slopes here, so proceed with care. Parties get lost here frequently during storms and whiteouts. The glacier is popular with ski mountaineers and telemarkers, despite the avalanche danger.

15 Camp Muir 🎿 ◆
Duration: 10-12 hrs

Situated at over 10,000 feet elevation, Camp Muir should be considered a mountaineering objective during winter and early spring. Prepare accordingly. The route is subject to high avalanche danger, and the weather can change very quickly. Parties have been stranded at Camp Muir for several days during winter and spring storms. Snow conditions often are difficult. Whiteout conditions make this a very dangerous descent. Be prepared to spend the night at Camp Muir, just in case the weather goes bad or you are not as fast as you thought you would be. Don't expect to ascend and descend in a single day unless conditions are perfect and you are a very strong skier and climber. This route has high avalanche danger in several places, so proceed with caution!

From Panorama Point, ascend the Muir Snowfield (Off-Trail Route 7), and ski back. The best early-season powder skiing is in October and November. Despite the dangers, if you are a skilled skier, this is one of the best early-season ski routes in the Pacific Northwest.

A solitary skier crosses a snow-covered glacier. (Photo: Mark Dale)

16 Van Trump Park
Duration: Overnight

Very experienced skiers can cross the Nisqually Glacier and ascend to the lower Wilson Glacier before descending across Van Trump Glaciers to Van Trump Park. This is highly-recommended telemarking country, but is not recommended except for very experienced backcountry skiers. Skiing out via Christine Falls is not recommended during winter, as it is steep and avalanche prone. In late spring, it is possible to hike in and out via Van Trump Park Trail. Overnight trips are common in this area, with basecamps below treeline recommended.

17 Tatoosh Range
Duration: 6-8 hrs

From Reflection Lakes, a fairly safe route ascends to the shoulder east of The Castle. The route is not completely protected from avalanches, but is recommended by many as the safest route to the crest. Don't try the route directly to Pinnacle-Plummer Saddle, as avalanche danger is very high. Some skiers aim for the divide between The Castle and Pinnacle Peak, which has increased exposure to avalanches. This is a wind deposit area, which has increased potential for avalanches.

Once at the crest of the Tatoosh Range, one can traverse in either direction as far as is feasible and safe. Foss Peak is a popular winter destination, reached via a relatively simple traverse to the east. A long slope south of the Castle's east shoulder is a popular ski descent, but sometimes avalanche-prone.

18 Box Canyon – Stevens Canyon Road 🎿 ■
Duration: Overnight

Begin from Stevens Canyon Entrance and ski to Box Canyon, an overnight tour with convenient and safe camping in the tunnel at Box Canyon. There is some avalanche danger along the east flank of Backbone Ridge. The portion of the road between Stevens Canyon Entrance and Box Canyon also is open for snowmobile use. Snowmobiles are not permitted past the tunnel, and because of very high avalanche danger, skiers should also stop here. It is possible, but not recommended, to ski from Paradise to Stevens Canyon Entrance.

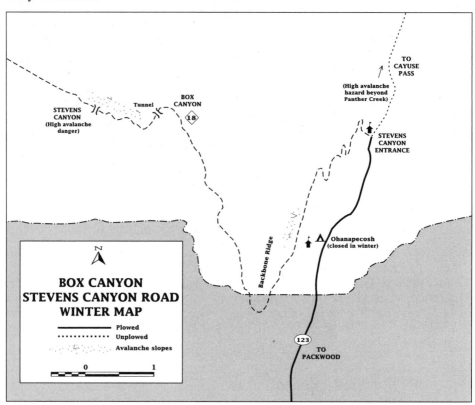

19 Chinook Pass 🎿 ● or ▲
Duration: 1-4 hrs

Chinook Pass has some highly-recommended early winter skiing. Highway 410 is closed during winter, so you should come before late October (in most years), following the first big snowstorm. If you wait too long, you'll miss it! If you do make it in time, the trail around Tipsoo Lake is suitable for less-able skiers. Those with more experience and ambition go for the orbit of Naches Peak, with opportunities for telemarking. In later season, the ski in via Highway 410 crosses several avalanche paths, making this a risky overnight trip.

20 White River Road

Duration: Overnight

White River Road is closed in winter, but is open to winter recreationalists, including snowmobilers, who may go as far as White River Campground. Begin from the Sno-Park (permit required) at the park entrance, and ski along the highway to White River Road. Continue to White River Campground. There is some avalanche danger along Highway 410 at Crystal and Deadwood Creeks, but little or none once past the White River entrance station. More-experienced skiers can continue into Glacier Basin, up Inter Glacier to Camp Schurman, or up to Sunrise and beyond. Snowmobilers may not continue up Highway 410 towards Cayuse Pass, nor up the Sunrise road. Skiers who venture to Cayuse Pass should be wary of avalanche slopes along the way.

In late spring, you can drive farther into the park, making approaches for many of the following trips much shorter.

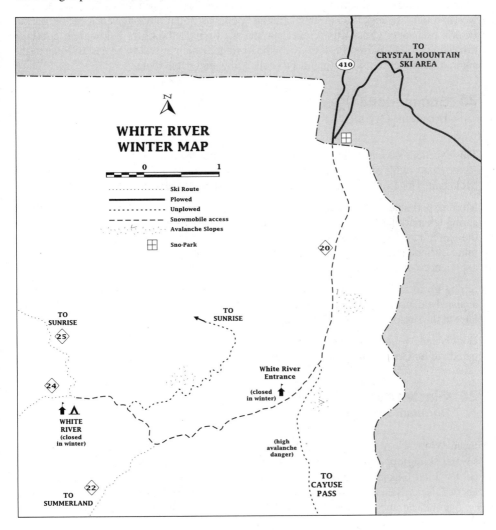

WHITE RIVER
WINTER MAP

0   1

.... Ski Route
————— Plowed
------------ Unplowed
— — — — Snowmobile access
Avalanche Slopes
⊞ Sno-Park

21 Tamanos Mountain 🎿 ▲
Duration: 6-8 hrs

Tamanos Mountain (6,790 ft/2070 m) is accessible from White River Road via the approximate route of Owyhigh Lakes Trail (Hike 24) and the off-trail route described in Chapter Six (Route 10). Beware of avalanche paths along the east side of the mountain; it is better to climb the ridge before Tamanos Creek during periods of avalanche danger. The summit is best left unclimbed by those without scrambling experience, especially when wet or snow covered. Best skied in early winter or spring, when the road is open.

22 Barrier Peak 🎿 🎿 ▲
Duration: 8-10 hrs

This trip is more feasible in late spring, when Cayuse Pass is open. From the pass, descend west through Sheepskull Gap, then contour southwest to an obvious bench below Barrier Peak's east face. Cross this cirque, staying well above the cliffs below, and continue traversing around Barrier Peak to its southeast ridge, which provides the easiest route to the summit. Experienced skiers find this a challenging, enjoyable route.

23 Summerland 🎿 🎿 ▲ or ◆
Duration: Overnight

This excellent ski tour follows the approximate path of the trail to Summerland from White River Road, with only a few potential avalanche areas along the slopes of Goat Island Mountain. This is a highly-recommended area for spring basecamp skiing.

More experienced skiers may continue up onto the Fryingpan Glacier for much-hyped spring telemarking (March through July recommended). Skiers have ascended to very near the summit of Little Tahoma Peak (via the climbing route described previously); this is more difficult and risky, and the summit climb should not be attempted in winter except by experienced mountaineers.

Skiing up to and on Fryingpan Glacier is a bad idea during periods of moderate or high avalanche danger. Wait until snow is very stable. Crevasses usually are not a problem until later in the season.

Goat Island Mountain is an easy spring snowshoe climb from Summerland, either from the gap dividing Goat Island from Little Tahoma or up one of its forested eastern ridges.

24 Glacier Basin – Inter Glacier 🎿 ■ or ◆
Duration: Overnight

From White River Campground, ski into Glacier Basin and set up base camp. There are several skiing opportunities here. Those with ambition can climb to Steamboat Prow and ski the Inter Glacier, a 4,000-foot descent. Because there is significant avalanche danger above Glacier Basin, you should not proceed unless snow conditions are perfect. Crevasses on Inter Glacier are well-filled by snowfall and avalanches, but use caution anyway.

25 Sunrise Area

Duration: Overnight

If you have come for solitude in a spectacular winter wonderland, Sunrise is one place to find it. The recommended route is to ascend the approximate line of the Wonderland Trail up from White River Campground. This is very steep, and you usually will fare better without skis. Once you reach Yakima Park, you'll be treated to pristine snow-covered meadows and wide-open views of Mount Rainier. Set up base camp, then ski along the crest of Sourdough Ridge, up to Burroughs Mountain (an excellent spring ski destination), or into Berkeley Park. There are a few avalanche slopes here and there, but most are avoided easily. The descent from Sunrise is best made along the road, although descending the creek drainage from Yakima Park to the first switchback below Sunrise Point is recommended.

Access is easier in spring, particularly when the road is open to near White River Campground.

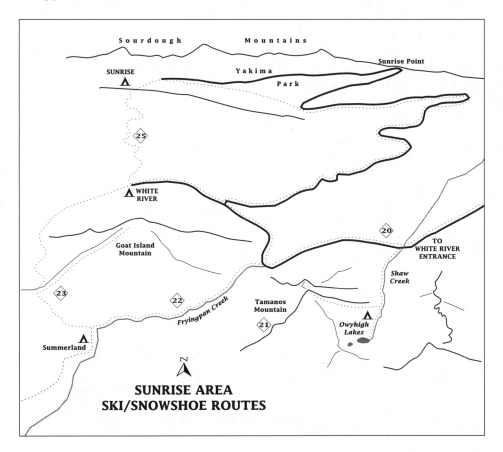

**SUNRISE AREA
SKI/SNOWSHOE ROUTES**

26 Grand Park ◆
Duration: 3-5 days

Grand Park is one of the most spectacular open meadows within Mount Rainier National Park, and in winter it is certainly the most remote. If you want solitude and scenery, Grand Park offers both. There are two possible ski routes into Grand Park. From Sunrise, follow the approximate route of the trail from Frozen Lake through Berkeley Park (Hike 31). This route crosses several avalanche slopes, particularly the slopes between Fremont Peak and Skyscraper Mountain. Experienced skiers should be able to reach Grand Park from Sunrise in a day.

The other route comes from outside the park via Road 73 (see Huckleberry Creek Trail, Hike 29), which now is gated near Highway 410 and thus a very long approach (but it's also free of snowmobile harassment). Ski the road, crossing avalanche tracks as quickly as possible. Head south into the park where the road passes Eleanor Creek. Navigate to Grand Park or Eleanor Lake, whichever you prefer. The lake offers more sheltered camping, but Grand Park is the recommended destination.

Grand Park is best reserved for experienced overnight skiers with considerable knowledge of avalanche safety, and winter routefinding and survival skills. Either way you approach Grand Park, expect to take a few days, and be prepared for bad weather. A grand tour would be to make a one-way loop via White River Road and Sunrise, then out via the Forest Service road – or the other way around.

27 Carbon River Road ⛷ ●
Duration: 4-6 hrs

If Carbon River Road continues to be closed from the park boundary during winter, skiers will have an easy route to Ipsut Creek Campground, provided there is sufficient snowfall. Its about 6 mi from the entrance to the campground, and very flat, with little elevation gain. There are plenty of campsites at Ipsut Creek, although there is no running water until the camground officially is opened later in the year.

28 Florence Peak 🚶 ■
Duration: 6-8 hrs

From the Carbon River entrance, hike the rainforest loop halfway and follow the East Boundary Trail (not maintained) some distance, past a small waterfall, to a divide, then traverse the ridge eastward to the summit of Florence Peak. Alternate routes are possible, and may be preferable if snow obscures the trail. This route has little avalanche danger, and is fairly easily accessed during witner. If snow conditions are good, you could cross Alki Crest to reach Tolmie Peak. Bring crampons and an ice ax, in case the upper ridge crest is crusty.

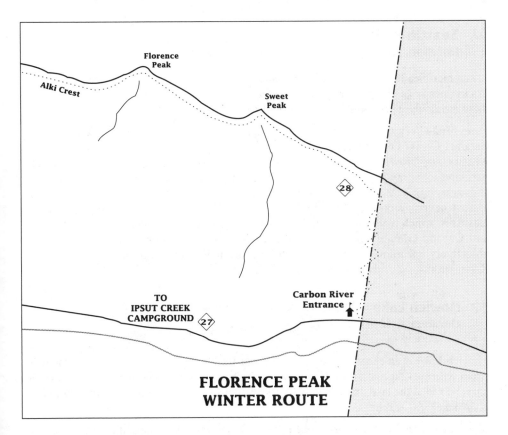

FLORENCE PEAK
WINTER ROUTE

29 Green Lake 🚶 ■
Duration: 4 hrs

The trail to Green Lake (Hike 32) offers snowshoeing through the old-growth forest. There is no avalanche danger along the trail, although snow falling from trees might get you!

30 Ipsut Creek 🚶 ■
Duration: 10 hrs

Snowshoers can make the 4 mi trip from Ipsut Creek Campground to Ipsut Pass via the approximate route of Ipsut Creek Trail (Hike 33). There is little avalanche danger until you get close to the big Alaska cedar tree, which is thus a good turnaround point.

31 Seattle Park ⛷ ◆
Duration: Overnight

In summer, Seattle Park is among the most scenic areas of Mount Rainier National Park. Rocky meadows creep over morainal ridges all the way up to the glaciers. In winter, these meadows are covered in snow, providing high and wild skiing.

From Ipsut Creek Campground, follow the approximate route of the Wonderland Trail to Cataract Creek. Once there, find a campsite that is sheltered from the wind. In poor weather, stay close to base camp so you can find it. You can tour across the wide-open parkland to Spray Park and back, or go telemarking on Flett and Russell Glaciers. Crevasses lurk here and there on Russell Glacier, so roping up is recommended (even if almost never practiced). Stay high on Russell Glacier to lessen your exposure to crevasses, which really open up lower down. Mavericks have descended Russell Glacier and Carbon Glacier on their way out to Ipsut Creek Campground; this is long, objectively hazardous, and may present a routefinding problem crossing the Carbon River, but it is very adventuresome.

32 Mowich Lake ⛷ 🚶 ■
Duration: 6-12 hrs

Mowich Lake is an excellent overnight ski tour for a novice. The route follows the road (from wherever the snow stops your car) to the lake, making routefinding very easy. On the road and at the lake, there is only a little avalanche danger. Campsites are easy to find at the lake. Stay off the lake!

Most skiers come in the spring, when the road is accessible to near the park boundary. Ski and snowshoe trips from base camp at Mowich Lake are numerous. Tolmie Peak is easily accessible, as are Knapsack Pass, Fay Peak and First Mother Mountain (although the final ascent to the summits of Fay Peak and Mother Mountain can be difficult and dangerous, especially when wet or snow-covered). There are avalanche areas on the slopes above Mowich Lake, so use caution.

33 Spray Park – Knapsack Pass ⛷ 🚶 ▲ or ◆
Duration: Overnight

From Mowich Lake, a winter climb over Knapsack Pass down to Spray Park is possible. Most follow the trail to Spray Park (Hike 38), which is easier and more protected from avalanches, but not as scenic. Knapsack Pass has higher objective danger than the trail route, but when snow and weather are stable, the views and the touring are worth the effort. Climb high onto the flanks of Observation Rock for telemarking, or tour across the vast parkland.

Base camp should be easy to find and sheltered from wind. It is very easy to get lost in a storm, so if poor weather moves in, get back to base camp fast.

34 Sunset Park

Duration: Overnight

Access to Sunset Park traditionally has involved skiing up the Westside Road, then following the Wonderland Trail another five miles to Golden Lakes – an involved affair with avalanche danger all along the road. Sunset Park has wide-open skiing with fantastic views of the mountain, but is not worth the trip from Westside Road. With the establishment of the Mt. Tahoma Scenic Ski Trail System across Champion International Corporation's land west of the park boundary, access to Sunset Park is now shorter and safer, making it a very accessible weekend tour up logging roads that come near the park boundary.

If you camp inside the park, you will need a backcountry permit; most camp just outside the boundary line to avoid this necessity.

A snowshoer enjoys the winter scape on Trail of the Shadows. (Photo: National Park Service)

Mt. Tahoma Scenic Ski Trails

As a compliment to all the fine skiing within Mount Rainier National Park is a network of maintained (but not groomed) trails located just outside the park's western boundary. Mt. Tahoma Scenic Ski Trails is a system of over 80 miles of established ski trails. These trails mostly follow logging roads, and are open to the public free of charge, except that a Sno-Park permit is required for trailhead parking, and a use permit is required for accessing Champion International Corp.'s land. The trails offer all levels of difficulty, with most of the trails being suited for advanced and expert skiers. As of winter 1990-91, one overnight hut is operational. When the remaining five huts are built, hut-to-hut skiing in Western Washington will be a reality.

Westside Road and part of the Wonderland Trail through Sunset Park are included in Mt. Tahoma Scenic Ski Trails. A map of the trail system is available locally. The trail system provides easy access to Sunset Park via Champion International Corp. land. A Backcountry Permit is required for overnight camping along the route within the park.

The trail system is administered by Mt. Tahoma Scenic Ski Trails Association, a non-profit organization. Skiers are encouraged to joint MTSSTA and to help support the trail system. For further information concerning membership, trails, access and huts, please contact MTSSTA, P.O. Box 942, Eatonville, WA 98328, (360) 847-8876.

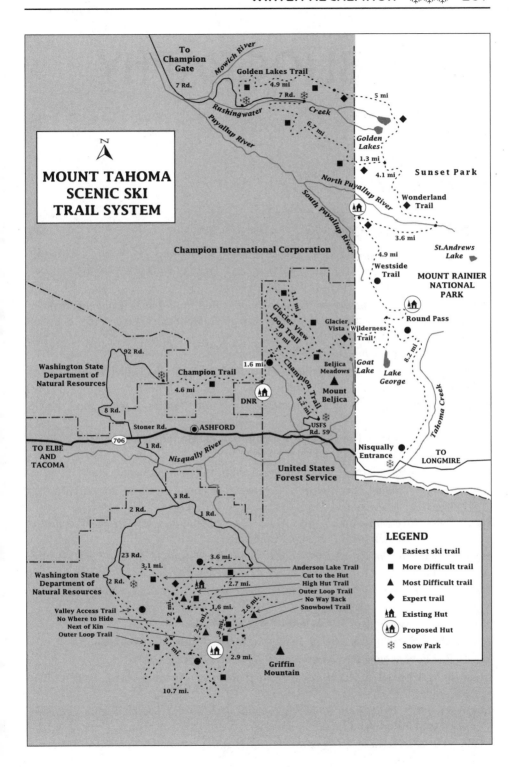

MOUNT TAHOMA
SCENIC SKI
TRAIL SYSTEM

To
Champion
Gate

7 Rd.

Mowich River

Golden Lakes Trail
4.9 mi

7 Rd.

Rushingwater   Creek

Puyallup River

6.7 mi

5 mi

Golden
Lakes

1.3 mi

4.1 mi   Sunset Park

North Puyallup River

Wonderland
Trail

3.6 mi

St. Andrews
Lake

Champion International Corporation

South Puyallup River

4.9 mi

Westside
Trail

MOUNT RAINIER
NATIONAL
PARK

92 Rd.

Washington State
Department of
Natural Resources

Champion Trail

4.6 mi

1.6 mi

Glacier View
Loop Trail
7.9 mi

1.1 mi

Glacier
Vista

Wilderness
Trail

Round Pass

8 Rd.

DNR

Champion Trail

3.2 mi

Beljica
Meadows

Mount
Beljica

Goat
Lake

Lake
George

8.2 mi

Tahoma Creek

Stoner Rd.   ASHFORD

706   1 Rd.

TO ELBE
AND
TACOMA

Nisqually River

USFS
Rd. 59

United States
Forest Service

Nisqually
Entrance

TO
LONGMIRE

3 Rd.

2 Rd.

1 Rd.

23 Rd.   3.6 mi.

3.1 mi.

2 Rd.

Washington State
Department of
Natural Resources

2.7 mi.

Anderson Lake Trail
Cut to the Hut
High Hut Trail
Outer Loop Trail
No Way Back
Snowbowl Trail

Valley Access Trail
No Where to Hide
Next of Kin
Outer Loop Trail

1.6 mi.

2.6 mi.

2.2 mi.

.8 mi.

2.9 mi.

Griffin
Mountain

10.7 mi.

LEGEND

● Easiest ski trail

■ More Difficult trail

▲ Most Difficult trail

◆ Expert trail

🏠 Existing Hut

🏠 Proposed Hut

❄ Snow Park

BIBLIOGRAPHY

BIBLIOGRAPHY

Key: (Date) 57: (page) 1–28, also 12/89:26–37.

Printed References:

American Alpine Journal. 36:475, 39:310, 49:143, 54:23, 57:1–28, 58:78–81, 59:301, 60:114–16, 61:336; 63:471, 64:169–70, 65:407, 66:128, 67:384–86, 69:305, 338–39, 71:228, 340, 72:114, 74:141–42, 79:184.

Beckey, F. 1987. *Cascade Alpine Guide, Climbing and High Routes, Columbia River to Stevens Pass* 2ed. Seattle: The Mountaineers; 1982. *Mountains of North America.* San Francisco: Sierra Club Books.

Bien 9/82. *Mountain Skiing.* Seattle: The Mountaineers.

Climbing (magazine). 5/82:15 (Basecamp: Little Tahoma Peak), 12/87:52–56 ("Willis Wall" by Gary Speer).

Crandell/ Mullineaux. "Volcanic Hazards at Mount Rainier, Washington." USGS Bulletin 1238.

Franklin, et al. 1988. The Forest Communities of Mount Rainier National Park. Scientific Monograph Series No. 19, USGPO.

Gillette/Dostal 1988: *Cross–Country Skiing,* 3ed., Seattle: The Mountaineers.

Haines 1962. *Mountain Fever, Historic Conquests of Rainier.* Salem: Oregon Historical Society.

Harris 1988. *Fire Mountains of the West: The Cascade and Mono Lake Volcanoes.* Missoula: Mountain Press Publishing Company.

Hazard, J. 1920. *The Glacier Playfields of Mount Rainier National Park.* Seattle: Western Printing.

Hazard, J. 1932. *Snow Sentinels of the Pacific Northwest.* Seattle: Lowman & Hanford Co.

Hoffman 1935. *Creation of Mount Rainier National Park.*

LaChapelle E.R. 1986: *The ABC of Avalanche Safety.* Seattle: The Mountaineers.

Lovitt, R. 12/89. *Around the Giant Mountain,* Backpacker magazine.

Manning/Spring 1975. *50 Hikes in Mount Rainier National Park.* Seattle: The Mountaineers.

Martinson 1986. *Wilderness Above the Sound: The Story of Mount Rainier National Park.* Seattle: Northland Press.

Mathews 1988. *Cascade – Olympic Natural History, a trailside reference.* Portland: Raven Editions.

Matthes 1928. *Mount Rainier and its Glaciers.*

Mazama (Club Journal). 00:1–40, 00:203–7, 05:201–34, 14:1–27, 19:301–18, 60:42–4.

Meany 1916. *Mount Rainier: A Record of Exploration.* Portland: Binfords & Mort.

Molenaar, D. 1987. *The Challenge of Rainier.* Seattle: The Mountaineers.

Mountaineer (Club Journal): 12:37, 18:49, 20:46–47, 24:57, 30:22–24, 31:12, 56–8, 33:14, 34:5, 35:3–7, 37:23, 38, 49:1–4, 55, 54:67–68, 56:38–54, 122, 58:96–99, 60:76, 61:97, 64:131, 69:112, 70:108–9, 71:72–74, 78:104.

Mountaineers, The 1990–91. *Mountaineering: Freedom of the Hills,* 4ed. Seattle: The Mountaineers 9/82; club trip reports, monthly club bulletins.

Nadeau 1983. *Highway to Paradise.* Tacoma: Valley Press.

National Geographic (Magazine) 5/63.

National Park Service. Mount Rainier National Park Wilderness Management Plan; Backcountry Trip Planner; Mount Rainier National Park press releases 1990–91; Hiker Information Center and Paradise Ranger Station resources; photo archive reviews, 1/91, 4/91.

Off Belay (Magazine): #1:22–26, #2:30–36, #13:4–9, 51, #18:2–9, #24:10–15, #29:2–5, #34:9–23, #35:21–25, #36:5–12, #42:2–9.

Prater 1988. *Snowshoeing,* 3ed. Seattle: The Mountaineers.

Ream 1983. *Northwest Volcanoes, A Roadside Geologic Guide.* Renton: B.J. Books.

Roper/Steck 1979. *Fifty Classic Climbs of North America.* San Francisco: Sierra Club Books.

Rusk C.E. 1924. *Tales of a Western Mountaineer.* Boston/New York: Houghton Mifflin Company (reprinted 1978, Seattle: The Mountaineers, with new photos and biography of C.E. Rusk by Darryl Lloyd).

Seattle Post–Intelligencer. 1/17/91:F1–2.

Seattle Times. 8/27/87:D1–2, 6/10/91:A1–2.

Selters A. 9/90. *Glacier Travel and Crevasse Rescue.* Seattle: The Mountaineers.

Sports Northwest (Magazine). 7/90, 5/91.

Steelquist 1987. *A traveler's companion to Mt. Rainier National Park.* Seattle: Pacific Northwest national parks and Forests Association.

Summit (Magazine). 1/57:10–11, 1/63:30–35, 7/66:8–11, 3/67:4–7, 9/71:16–17, 5/72:6–8, 5/73:2–7, 7/86:4–6.

Tolbert 1933. *History of Mount Rainier National Park.* Seattle: Lowman & Hanford.

Veatch 1969. "Analysis of a 24–year Record of Nisqually Glacier," USGS Bulletin.

Washington Trails Association. TRIS computer trail database.

Wilkerson J. 1986. *Medicine for Mountaineering.* Seattle: The Mountaineers.

Wilkerson/Bangs/Hayward 1986. *Hypothermia, Frostbite and Other Cold Injuries.* Seattle: The Mountaineers.

Personal References:

Attaway, Joel: Interviews and correspondence, manuscript review (ski routes) 2/91, 3/91.

Berry, Howard: Telephone interview (alpine scrambles) 12/90.

Curran, Dick: Telephone interview (ski routes) 5/91.

Dale, Mark: Telephone interview, correspondence, photo review, manuscript review (climbing and ski routes) 12/90.

Dixson, John: Telephone interview (bicycling) 5/91.

Dietz, Bob: Telephone interview (ski routes) 5/91.

Doty, Steve: Telephone interview (climbing routes) 5/91.

Driggers, Dorthea: Telephone interview (alpine scrambles) 5/91.

Duggan, John: Interview (bicycling) 4/91.

Emetaz, Roland: Correspondence, manuscript review (winter travel) 4/91.

Erschler, Phil: Correspondence, manuscript review (climbing routes) 2/90.

Gentry, Pat: Interviews, correspondence, photo reviews (hiking and alpine scrambles) 9/90, 1/91.

Hentges, Cy: Interviews and correspondence (park regulations and policy) 4/91, 6/91.

Jordan, Marty: Telephone interview (alpine scrambles) 7/91.

Lepeska, Dan: Interview (climbing routes) 6/86.

Lovitt, Rob: Interview, photo review (Wonderland Trail) 11/90.

Molenaar, Dee: Correspondence and interview, manuscript review (climbing routes) 3/90.

Nielsen, Larry: Correspondence, manuscript review (climbing routes) 2/90.

Olsen, Jon: Interview, photo review (climbing and skiing routes) 5/91.

Olsen, Sue: Telephone interview (snowshoeing routes) 5/91.

Olson, Garry: Correspondence, manuscript review (climbing routes) 9/90.

Ostrowski, Dan: Interviews and correspondence (hiking and climbing routes) 4/91–8/91.

Pommert, Jim: Telephone interview (alpine scrambles) 4/91.

Rankin, Dale: Telephone interview (alpine scrambles) 5/91.

Samora, Barbara: Interviews and correspondence, manuscript review (park regulations and policy) 4/91, 5/91.

Schmidt, Don: Telephone interview (alpine scrambles) 5/91.

Smith, Kurt: Photo review (climbing routes) 8/90.

Weaver, Doug: Interviews and correspondence, manuscript review (hiking, climbing routes) 9/90, 8/91.

Weaver, Howard: Interviews and correspondence, manuscript review, photo review (climbing routes) 3/91, 4/91.

Wickwire, James: Correspondence, manuscript review (climbing routes) 2/90.

Wilkerson, Tod: Interview (climbing routes) 5/82.

Yates, Margaret: Interviews and correspondence, manuscript review (park regulations and policy) 12/90, 3/91, 4/91.

Map References:

Mt. Rainier National Park visitors map (NPS).

Mt. Rainier National Park, USGS 1:50,000–scale topographic map.

USGS 15 Minute Series: Bumping Lake.

USGS 7 Minute Series: Golden Lakes, Mount Wow, Mowich Lake, Mount Rainier West, Mount Rainier East, Sunrise, White River Park, Chinook Pass.

"Mount Rainier National Park, Washington," oblique–view pictorial landform map (Molenaar's 1986 revision).

"Hiking Map & Guide, Mount Rainier National Park," Eureka, California: Earthwalk Press 9/90 (1:50,000 scale topographic map).

Green Trails 15 Minute Series: No. 269 ("Mt. Rainier West, Wash."), No. 270 ("Mt. Rainier East, Wash."), No. 270S ("Paradise, Wash."), P.O. Box 1271, Bellevue, WA 98009.

Trails Illustrated: Topo No. 217 ("Mount Rainier National Park"), Evergreen, Colorado. (Topographic 1:50,000 scale, provides additional information not contained on USGS maps; and is a good, weather–resistant substitute).

USGS Photographs:

United States Geological Survey photographs used in this guide were obtained from Dave Hirst of the USGS Ice and Climate Project, University of Puget Sound, Tacoma, Washington 98416.

The following USGS photographs of Mount Rainier were used in this guide: 69R1–50, 69R1–70, 69R1–74, 69R1–76, 69R1–81, 67L8–58, 67L8–76, F648–160, F648–161, all by Austin Post.

Guide Services:

Rainier Mountaineering, Inc. is the park's sole climbing guide concessionaire. However, all of the following guide services presently have incidental business permits to conduct guided climbs of Mount Rainier. This list is subject to change; check the Mount Rainier National Park homepage for current listings, or call or write these guide services for further information.

Alpine Ascents International
121 Mercer Street
Seattle, WA 98109
(206) 378-1927

American Alpine Institute

1515 12th Street
Bellingham, WA 98225
(360) 671-1505

Cascade Alpine Guides
P.O. Box 40563
Bellevue, WA 98015-4563
(425) 688-8054

Mount Rainier Alpine Guides
P.O. Box "T"
Ashford, WA 98304
(360) 569-0977

Rainier Mountaineering, Inc.
535 Dock Street, Suite 209
Tacoma, WA 98402

Websites

The following sites on the World Wide Web provide useful information and links to other Mount Rainier National Park websites.

www.npw.gov/mora/ (official Mount Rainier National Park homepage, including updated weather, road, trail and climbing route information).

www.halcyon.com/rdpayne/mrnp.html (unofficial Mount Rainier National Park website, with links to other sites).

www.seainfo.noaa.gov/cgi-bin/zone.cgi?18 (current weather forecast for western slopes of the central Cascades and extended forecast for western Washington).

www.nwac.noaa.gov/ (avalanche forecasts for Washington and northern Oregon, mountain weather data, etc.).

Camping and Lodging

For campsite reservations at Cougar Rock and Ohanapecosh, contact:

National Park Reservation Service
P.O. Box 1600
Cumberland, MD 21502
1-800-365-CAMP (2267)
Fax 1-301-722-1174

For reservations at the National Park Inn or Paradise Inn, contact:

Mount Rainier Guest Services, Inc.
P.O. Box 108
Ashford, WA 98304
(360) 569-2275